The Fountain Within

The Fountain Within

Praying St John's Gospel

Introduced and edited by
ROBERT LLEWELYN

Darton, Longman and Todd
London

First published in 1989 by
Darton, Longman and Todd Ltd
89 Lillie Road, London SW6 1UD

Introduction and edition
© 1989 Robert Llewelyn

The translation of St John's Gospel is taken from
the New Jerusalem Bible published and copyright © 1985
by Darton, Longman and Todd Ltd and Doubleday & Co Inc
and is used by permission of the publishers

British Library Cataloguing in Publication Data

The Fountain within.
1. Bible. N.T. John. Devotional works
I. Llewelyn, Robert   II. [Bible. N.T. John.
English. New Jerusalem, 1985]
242'.5

ISBN 0–232–51831–9

All royalties earned by the sale of
this book are being given to
The Julian Shrine, c/o All Hallows,
Rouen Road, Norwich

Phototypeset by Input Typesetting Ltd
London SW19 8DR

Printed and bound in Great Britain by
Anchor Press Ltd, Tiptree, Essex

CONTENTS

INTRODUCTION

This book is intended for individual and corporate use. Its purpose is to assist the reader (or the group) to stand before the Scriptures with the critical faculties stilled, allowing them to make what impact they will. It is doubtless best tested at the personal level before being introduced to a group.

This is to be the time when the Scriptures are to be given the chance to speak at a deeper than conscious level; our part is to be receptive in their presence. The mind is largely passive, the heart open to what God may give. To make a deliberate effort at reflection would be likely to stand in the way of receptivity at the levels of personality which these readings are designed to reach. If, however, reflections come, we are to accept them; yet we are not deliberately to enlarge on them but, rather, to be content to rest with them in God. The active examination of the text is not unimportant but it belongs to another time. Readers who persevere with the method of this book will almost certainly find themselves searching out commentaries later on.*

Many know what it is to listen to the Epistle and Gospel in church in some such way. But then, as soon as they are over, we are taken to something else and miss the benefit which silence might bring. Such silence, if it were observed, might simply be the occasion for the expression of our desire for God; simply to desire God *is* to pray, whether it feels that way or not. Or, more passively, the silence might be the occasion for resting in the love of God – however the call may be at the time – allowing him to work as he will.

So should it be in these meditations. Perhaps later there will be just a hazy memory, or none at all, of what has been read. That will not matter: we have been fed and that is enough; we shall continue to be nourished until our next meal. And with faithful practice the rich symbolism of the Gospel will come to

---

* For this purpose William Temple's *Readings in St John's Gospel* (London, Macmillan 1940) is highly recommended. See also page 90n for particulars of William Barclay's commentary on St John's Gospel.

be stored in the heart, to be quickened by the fountain of living water of which it speaks.

The meditations are intended to be used; a casual perusal will not help. When used alone, a time of not less than ten minutes is suggested. A fifteen- or twenty-minute period can pass very quickly with the readings and silences split up as indicated, and some readers will opt for half an hour. On some days the silence may take over and the book, which is but an instrument, should be laid aside.

The total time of the meditation will clearly depend chiefly on the times given to the silences, making the reading adjustable in corporate use to, say, the needs of a family, a circle of friends or a Quiet Day in church. If the silences are as short as fifteen seconds, the total time will be about six minutes; if they are as long as five minutes, then the whole will take about half an hour. A further adjustment can be made by combining readings, in which case the number of silences will of course be correspondingly reduced.

A glance at the pages will reveal a common pattern throughout the book. At the heart of each portion are five readings on a selected gospel theme followed by a refrain and silence. The refrain which follows each reading may be said as a versicle and response, or by the leader alone, or by all. If it is felt that the silence is impaired, then the refrain can be omitted altogether.

It will be seen that whilst the refrain set is common throughout the book, an alternative refrain is offered at the end of each portion. Some readers will prefer the same refrain daily, since it will then become as a well-loved prayer, lodged in the heart, which may speak of its own accord through the day. Others may like to explore the refrains scattered as tailpieces throughout the book and select one or more for frequent use.

The translation is that of the New Jerusalem Bible and it is hoped that these selections, which cover almost the whole of St John's Gospel, may have ecumenical appeal. If so, a number of readers will be acquainted with the rosary and some may like to fill the silences with its use, employing the refrain offered or an alternative of their choice. For many the rosary is a help to raising the soul to God or relaxing into God – we shall know at the time how it should be. The five silences correspond to the five decades.

The dedication of this book to Our Lady of Medjugorje may call for expansion. My own closeness to Medjugorje is in a spiritual sense only, not least through the treasured gift of a rosary linked by local blessing to the heart of its life. The message of Medjugorje is peace, peace in our hearts, peace in reconciliation with one another, peace in society, and all the way to peace among nations. The call comes through six young people (and two other children, see p. 101) to whom since 1981 has been granted a series of visions in which Christ's Mother appears to them, and speaks with them and they with her. The messages, though not all can yet be revealed, are simple and plain ('Listen to my Son', 'Pray, pray, pray'), though clearly if they were generally obeyed they would be earthshaking in their consequences. The heart of the teaching lies in the call to renewal of life through repentance and prayer, but with the corollary that apart from a widespread turning to God cata-strophic events must overtake our troubled world. This prophecy is to be seen as a statement of fact and not a threat for, to quote again, 'The only attitude of the Christian towards the future is hope of salvation . . . If you think about evil, punishment, war, you are on the road towards them. Your task is to accept Divine Peace, to live it and spread it.' And if I may expand the message quoted on prayer: 'When I say: pray, pray, pray, do not understand it as meaning only an increase in the number of your prayers. I want to bring you to a deep desire for God, a continuous desire for God.' Remarkable healing miracles have on occasions followed the appearances, long-standing feuds have been healed, families reconciled and the faith of many strengthened or renewed.

I dare to believe that this remote, communist-governed Yugoslavian village, to which more than ten million people have been drawn since the visions began, has been chosen by God to present to the world the most important and significant message of our time. Summit conferences and the rest, how-ever important in their own sphere, do but scratch at the surface of events, whereas in this place and in all places in spiritual association with it, we are brought face to face with the forces at the heart of reality. Any who wish to know more of the strange and persistent happenings touched upon here only in the barest outline would do well to read Mary Craig's timely and objectively researched book *Spark from*

Heaven.* It is only fair to say that whilst the author hopes the events will be proved to be authentic, her own mind remains open. So, too, does the official mind of the Catholic Church, though many clergy and others – medical and other professional investigators among them – have no doubt of their veracity

To end on a practical note: individual users of this book will know which posture suits them best. But where the readings are used corporately, it is suggested that it will be best to sit throughout. Most people in the West now like to sit for silent prayer. Richard Rolle, the father of the English mystics, had some lovely words to say about sitting: 'Sitting, I am most at rest and my heart most upward. I have loved to sit, for thus I have loved God more, and I remained longer within the comfort of love than if I were walking or standing or kneeling.' So may it be for those who use these readings!

ROBERT LLEWELYN
The Julian Shrine
c/o All Hallows
Rouen Road
Norwich

* See Mary Craig, *Spark from Heaven* (London, Hodder & Stoughton 1988).

Dedicated to

Our Lady of Medjugorje

who

*through her spiritual children
is pleading that the world
may listen to her Son*

Pray for us

When wilt thou come, Jesu my Joy,
  and rescue me from woe;
And give thyself to me, and be
  with me for ever so.
All my desires would be fulfilled
  if that were given to me;
All my desires are one desire,
  and that for naught but thee.
  Richard Rolle

The coming of the Word

John 1:1–18

In the name of the Father, and of the Son, and of the Holy Spirit. Amen.

Our Father . . .

In the beginning was the Word: the Word was with God and the Word was God. He was with God in the beginning. Through him all things came into being, not one thing came into being except him. What has come into being in him was life, life that was the light of men; and light shines in darkness, and darkness could not overpower it.

> *Blessed be Jesus, true God and true man.*
> *Blessed be the name of Jesus.*

SILENCE

A man came, sent by God. His name was John. He came as a witness, to bear witness to the light, so that everyone might believe through him. He was not the light, he was to bear witness to the light.

REFRAIN FOLLOWED BY SILENCE

The Word was the real light that gives light to everyone; he was coming into the world. He was in the world that had come into being through him, and the world did not recognise him. He came to his own and his own people did not accept him. But to those who did accept him he gave power to become children of God, to those who believed in his name who were born not from human stock or human desire or human will but from God himself.

REFRAIN FOLLOWED BY SILENCE

The Word became flesh, he lived among us, and we saw his glory, the glory that he has from the Father as only Son of the Father, full of grace and truth.

REFRAIN FOLLOWED BY SILENCE

John witnesses to him. He proclaims, 'This is the one of whom I said: He who comes after me has passed ahead of me because he existed before me.' Indeed, from his fullness we have, all of us, received – one gift replacing another, for the Law was given through Moses, grace and truth have come through Jesus Christ. No one has ever seen God; it is the only Son, who is close to the Father's heart, who has made him known.

REFRAIN FOLLOWED BY SILENCE

Glory to the Father, and to the Son, and to the Holy Spirit: as it was in the beginning, is now, and shall be for ever.   Amen.

Father, through the coming of your Son you have banished the darkness of this world and brought light to your people. We ask you to drive from us the darkness of sin and to enlighten our hearts with the glory of your grace, which you have given us in your Son, our Lord and Saviour Jesus Christ.   Amen.

ALTERNATIVE REFRAIN:
> *The Word was made flesh and dwelt among us:*
> *And we beheld his glory, full of grace and truth.*

The witness of John the Baptist

John 1:19–39

In the name of the Father, and of the Son, and of the Holy Spirit. Amen.

Our Father . . .

This was the witness of John, when the Jews sent to him priests and Levites from Jerusalem to ask him, 'Who are you?' He declared, he did not deny but declared, 'I am not the Christ.' So they asked, 'Then are you Elijah?' He replied, 'I am not.' 'Are you the Prophet?' He answered, 'No.' So they said to him, 'Who are you? We must take back an answer to those who sent us. What have you to say about yourself?' So he said, 'I am, as Isaiah prophesied: A voice of one that cries in the desert: Prepare a way for the Lord. Make his paths straight!'

Blessed be Jesus, true God and true man.
Blessed be the name of Jesus.

SILENCE

Now those who had been sent were Pharisees, and they put this question to him, 'Why are you baptising if you are not the Christ, and not Elijah, and not the Prophet?' John answered them, 'I baptise with water; but standing among you – unknown to you – is the one who is coming after me; and I am not fit to undo the strap of his sandal.' This happened at Bethany, on the far side of the Jordan, where John was baptising.

REFRAIN FOLLOWED BY SILENCE

The next day, he saw Jesus coming towards him and said, 'Look, there is the lamb of God that takes away the sin of the world. It was of him that I said, "Behind me comes one who has passed ahead of me because he existed before me." I did not know him myself, and yet my purpose in coming to baptise with water was so that he might be revealed to Israel.'

REFRAIN FOLLOWED BY SILENCE

4

And John declared, 'I saw the Spirit come down on him like a dove from heaven and rest on him. I did not know him myself, but he who sent me to baptise with water had said to me, "The man on whom you see the Spirit come down and rest is the one who is to baptise with the Holy Spirit." I have seen and I testify that he is the Chosen One of God.'

REFRAIN FOLLOWED BY SILENCE

The next day as John stood there again with two of his disciples, Jesus went past, and John looked towards him and said, 'Look, there is the lamb of God.' And the two disciples heard what he said and followed Jesus. Jesus turned round, saw them following and said, 'What do you want?' They answered, 'Rabbi' – which means Teacher – 'where do you live?' He replied, 'Come and see'; so they went and saw where he lived, and stayed with him that day. It was about the tenth hour.

REFRAIN FOLLOWED BY SILENCE

Glory to the Father, and to the Son, and to the Holy Spirit: as it was in the beginning, is now, and shall be for ever.   Amen.

Lord, we too would stay with you: enable us to remain with you, faithful to the end.   Amen.

ALTERNATIVE REFRAIN:
It is the Spirit that bears witness:
Because the Spirit is truth.

The first disciples

John 1:40–51

In the name of the Father, and of the Son, and of the Holy Spirit. Amen.

Our Father . . .

One of these two who became followers of Jesus after hearing what John had said was Andrew, the brother of Simon Peter. The first thing Andrew did was to find his brother and say to him, 'We have found the Messiah' – which means the Christ – and he took Simon to Jesus. Jesus looked at him and said, 'You are Simon son of John; you are to be called Cephas' – which means Rock.

> *Blessed be Jesus, true God and true man.*
> *Blessed be the name of Jesus.*

SILENCE

The next day, after Jesus had decided to leave for Galilee, he met Philip and said, 'Follow me.' Philip came from the same town, Bethsaida, as Andrew and Peter. Philip found Nathaniel and said to him, 'We have found him of whom Moses in the Law and the prophets wrote, Jesus son of Joseph, from Nazareth.' Nathaniel said to him, 'From Nazareth? Can anything good come from that place?' Philip replied, 'Come and see.'

REFRAIN FOLLOWED BY SILENCE

When Jesus saw Nathaniel coming he said of him, 'There, truly, is an Israelite in whom there is no deception.' Nathaniel asked, 'How do you know me?' Jesus replied, 'Before Philip came to call you, I saw you under the fig tree.'

REFRAIN FOLLOWED BY SILENCE

Nathaniel answered, 'Rabbi, you are the Son of God, you are the king of Israel.' Jesus replied, 'You believe that just because

I said: I saw you under the fig tree. You are going to see greater things than that.'

REFRAIN FOLLOWED BY SILENCE

And then he added, 'In all truth I tell you, you will see heaven open and the angels of God ascending and descending over the Son of man.'

REFRAIN FOLLOWED BY SILENCE

Glory to the Father, and to the Son, and to the Holy Spirit: as it was in the beginning, is now, and shall be for ever.   Amen.

Grant to us, Lord, such purity of heart, that we may know ourselves without deception, and worship you in gladness and truth.   Amen.

ALTERNATIVE REFRAIN:
> *Blessed are the pure in heart:*
> *For they shall see God.*

The wedding at Cana

John 2:1–12

In the name of the Father, and of the Son, and of the Holy Spirit. Amen.

Our Father . . .

On the third day there was a wedding at Cana in Galilee. The mother of Jesus was there, and Jesus and his disciples had also been invited.

> *Blessed be Jesus, true God and true man.*
> *Blessed be the name of Jesus.*

SILENCE

And they ran out of wine, since the wine provided for the feast had all been used, and the mother of Jesus said to him, 'They have no wine.' Jesus said, 'Woman, what do you want from me? My hour has not come yet.'

REFRAIN FOLLOWED BY SILENCE

His mother said to the servants, '*Do whatever he tells you.*' There were six stone water-jars standing there, meant for the ablutions that are customary among the Jews: each could hold twenty or thirty gallons. Jesus said to the servants, 'Fill the jars with water,' and they filled them to the brim.

REFRAIN FOLLOWED BY SILENCE

Then he said to them, 'Draw some out now and take it to the president of the feast.' They did this; the president tasted the water, and it had turned into wine. Having no idea where it came from – though the servants who had drawn the water knew – the president of the feast called the bridegroom and said, 'Everyone serves good wine first and the worse wine when the guests are well-wined; but you have kept the best wine till now.'

REFRAIN FOLLOWED BY SILENCE

This was the first of Jesus' signs: it was at Cana in Galilee. He revealed his glory, and his disciples believed in him. After this he went down to Capernaum with his mother and his brothers and his disciples, but they stayed there only a few days.

REFRAIN FOLLOWED BY SILENCE

Glory to the Father, and to the Son, and to the Holy Spirit: as it was in the beginning, is now, and shall be for ever.   Amen.

Lord, in your love you blessed a wedding in Cana. We ask your blessing on our homes and families. Help us to know the strength and joy which come from you, and may your peace rule our hearts.   Amen.

ALTERNATIVE REFRAIN:
O give thanks unto the Lord, for he is gracious:
And his mercy endures for ever.

The cleansing of the Temple

John 2:13–25

In the name of the Father, and of the Son, and of the Holy Spirit. Amen.

Our Father . . .

When the time of the Jewish Passover was near Jesus went up to Jerusalem, and in the Temple he found people selling cattle and sheep and doves, and the money changers sitting there.

> *Blessed be Jesus, true God and true man.*
> *Blessed be the name of Jesus.*

SILENCE

Making a whip out of cord, he drove them all out of the Temple, sheep and cattle as well, scattered the money changers' coins, knocked their tables over and said to the dove-sellers, 'Take all this out of here and stop using my Father's house as a market.' Then his disciples remembered the words of scripture: *I am eaten up with zeal for your house.*

REFRAIN FOLLOWED BY SILENCE

The Jews intervened and said, 'What sign can you show us that you should act like this?' Jesus answered, 'Destroy this Temple, and in three days I will raise it up.' The Jews replied, 'It has taken forty-six years to build this Temple: are you going to raise it up again in three days?'

REFRAIN FOLLOWED BY SILENCE

But he was speaking of the Temple that was his body, and when Jesus rose from the dead, his disciples remembered that he had said this, and they believed the scripture and what he had said.

REFRAIN FOLLOWED BY SILENCE

During his stay in Jerusalem for the feast of the Passover many believed in his name when they saw the signs that he did, but Jesus knew all people and did not trust himself to them; he never needed evidence about anyone; he could tell what someone had in him.

REFRAIN FOLLOWED BY SILENCE

Glory to the Father, and to the Son, and to the Holy Spirit: as it was in the beginning, is now, and shall be for ever.   Amen.

You, Lord, who cleansed the Temple, cleanse, too, our hearts that they may be the temple of the Holy Spirit.   Amen.

ALTERNATIVE REFRAIN:
> *The Lord whom you seek:*
> *Shall come suddenly into his Temple.*

You must be born from above

John: 3:1–21

In the name of the Father, and of the Son, and of the Holy Spirit. Amen.

Our Father . . .

There was one of the Pharisees called Nicodemus, a leader of the Jews, who came to Jesus by night and said, 'Rabbi, we know that you have come from God as a teacher; for no one could perform the signs that you do unless God were with him.' Jesus answered, 'In all truth I tell you, no one can see the kingdom of God without being born from above.'

> *Blessed be Jesus, true God and true man.*
> *Blessed be the name of Jesus.*

SILENCE

Nicodemus said, 'How can anyone who is already old be born? Is it possible to go back into the womb again and be born?' Jesus replied, 'In all truth I tell you, no one can enter the kingdom of God without being born through water and the Spirit; what is born of human nature is human; what is born of the Spirit is spirit. Do not be surprised when I say: You must be born from above. The wind blows where it pleases; you can hear its sound, but you cannot tell where it comes from or where it is going. So it is with everyone who is born of the Spirit.'

REFRAIN FOLLOWED BY SILENCE

'How is that possible?' asked Nicodemus. Jesus replied, 'You are the Teacher of Israel, and you do not know these things! In all truth I tell you, we speak only about what we know and witness only to what we have seen and yet you people reject our evidence. If you do not believe me when I speak to you about earthly things, how will you believe me when I speak to you about heavenly things? No one has gone up to heaven except the one who came down from heaven, the Son of man; as Moses lifted up the snake in the desert, so must the Son of

man be lifted up so that everyone who believes may have
eternal life in him. For this is how God loved the world: he
gave his only Son, so that everyone who believes in him may
not perish but may have eternal life.'

REFRAIN FOLLOWED BY SILENCE

'For God sent his Son into the world not to judge the world,
but so that through him the world might be saved. No one
who believes in him will be judged; but whoever does not
believe is judged already, because that person does not believe
in the Name of God's only Son.'

REFRAIN FOLLOWED BY SILENCE

'And the judgement is this: though the light has come into the
world people have preferred darkness to the light because their
deeds were evil. And indeed, everybody who does wrong
hates the light and avoids it, to prevent his actions from being
shown up; but whoever does the truth comes out into the
light, so that what he is doing may plainly appear as done in
God.'

REFRAIN FOLLOWED BY SILENCE

Glory to the Father, and to the Son, and to the Holy Spirit: as
it was in the beginning, is now, and shall be for ever.   Amen.

Spirit of the living God, inspire the hearts of your people, and
kindle within them the fire of your love.   Amen.

ALTERNATIVE REFRAIN:
> *Come, Holy Ghost, our souls inspire:*
> *And lighten with celestial fire.*

John the Baptist proclaims the Christ

John 3:22–36

In the name of the Father, and of the Son, and of the Holy Spirit. Amen.

Our Father . . .

After this, Jesus went with his disciples into the Judaean countryside and stayed with them there and baptised. John also was baptising at Aenon near Salim, where there was plenty of water, and people were going there and were being baptised. For John had not yet been put in prison.

> *Blessed be Jesus, true God and true man.*
> *Blessed be the name of Jesus.*

SILENCE

Now a discussion arose between some of John's disciples and a Jew about purification, so they went to John and said, 'Rabbi, the man who was with you on the far side of the Jordan, the man to whom you bore witness, is baptising now, and everyone is going to him. John replied, 'No one can have anything except what is given him from heaven. You yourselves can bear me out. I said, "I am not the Christ; I am the one who has been sent to go in front of him." '

REFRAIN FOLLOWED BY SILENCE

'It is the bridegroom who has the bride; and yet the bridegroom's friend, who stands there and listens to him, is filled with joy at the bridegroom's voice. This is the joy I feel, and it is complete. He must grow greater, I must grow less.'

REFRAIN FOLLOWED BY SILENCE

He who comes from above is above all others; he who is of the earth is earthly himself and speaks in an earthly way. He who comes from heaven bears witness to the things he has seen and heard, but his testimony is not accepted by anybody; though anyone who does accept his testimony is attesting that

God is true, since he whom God has sent speaks God's own words, for God gives him the Spirit without reserve.'

REFRAIN FOLLOWED BY SILENCE

(John continued): 'The Father loves the Son and has entrusted everything to his hands. Anyone who believes in the Son has eternal life, but anyone who refuses to believe in the Son will never see life: God's retribution hangs over him.'

REFRAIN FOLLOWED BY SILENCE

Glory to the Father, and to the Son, and to the Holy Spirit: as it was in the beginning, is now, and shall be for ever.   Amen.

Grant, Lord, that our lives may be so grounded in truth that we take not for ourselves what belongs to you, for yours is the kingdom, the power and the glory.   Amen.

ALTERNATIVE REFRAIN:
> *The Father loves the Son:*
> *And has given all things into his hands.*

Come, everyone who thirsts

John 4:1–26

In the name of the Father, and of the Son, and of the Holy Spirit. Amen.

Our Father . . .

When Jesus heard that the Pharisees had found out that he was making and baptising more disciples than John – though in fact it was his disciples who baptised, not Jesus himself – he left Judaea and went back to Galilee. He had to pass through Samaria. On the way he came to the Samaritan town called Sychar near the land that Jacob gave to his son Joseph. Jacob's well was there and Jesus, tired by the journey, sat down by the well. It was about the sixth hour.

> *Blessed be Jesus, true God and true man.*
> *Blessed be the name of Jesus.*

SILENCE

When a Samaritan woman came to draw water, Jesus said to her, 'Give me something to drink.' His disciples had gone into the town to buy food. The Samaritan woman said to him, 'You are a Jew. How is it that you ask me, a Samaritan, for something to drink?' – Jews, of course, do not associate with Samaritans. Jesus replied to her, 'If you only knew what God is offering and who it is that is saying to you, "Give me something to drink," you would have been the one to ask, and he would have given you living water.'

REFRAIN FOLLOWED BY SILENCE

'You have no bucket, sir,' she answered, 'and the well is deep: how do you get this living water? Are you a greater man than our father Jacob, who gave us this well and drank from it himself with his sons and his cattle?' Jesus replied, 'Whoever drinks this water will be thirsty again; but no one who drinks the water that I shall give him will ever be thirsty again: the water that I shall give him will become in him a spring of water, welling up for eternal life.'

REFRAIN FOLLOWED BY SILENCE

16

'Sir,' said the woman, 'give me some of that water, so that I may never be thirsty or come here again to draw water.' 'Go and call your husband,' said Jesus to her, 'and come back here.' The woman answered, 'I have no husband.' Jesus said to her, 'You are right to say, "I have no husband"; for although you have had five, the one you now have is not your husband. You spoke the truth there.' 'I see you are a prophet, sir,' said the woman. 'Our fathers worshipped on this mountain, though you say that Jerusalem is the place where one ought to worship.'

REFRAIN FOLLOWED BY SILENCE

Jesus said, 'Believe me, woman, the hour is coming when you will worship the Father neither on this mountain nor in Jerusalem. You worship what you do not know; we worship what we do know; for salvation comes from the Jews. But the hour is coming – indeed is already here – when true worshippers will worship the Father in spirit and truth: that is the kind of worshipper the Father seeks. God is Spirit, and those who worship must worship in spirit and truth.' The woman said to him, 'I know that Messiah – that is, Christ – is coming; and when he comes he will explain everything.' Jesus said, 'That is who I am, I who speak to you.'

REFRAIN FOLLOWED BY SILENCE

Glory to the Father, and to the Son, and to the Holy Spirit: as it was in the beginning, is now, and shall be for ever.   Amen.

Be to us, Lord, as a spring of living water, cleansing and refreshing us for your service.   Amen.

ALTERNATIVE REFRAIN:
> *If any man thirst:*
> *Let him come to me and drink.*

Seedtime and harvest

John 4:27–42

In the name of the Father, and of the Son, and of the Holy Spirit. Amen.

Our Father . . .

At this point his disciples returned and were surprised to find him speaking to a woman, though none of them asked, 'What do you want from her?' or, 'What are you talking to her about?' The woman put down her water-jar and hurried back to the town to tell the people, 'Come and see a man who has told me everything I have done; could this be the Christ?' This brought people out of the town and they made their way towards him.

Blessed be Jesus, true God and true man.
Blessed be the name of Jesus.

SILENCE

Meanwhile, the disciples were urging him, 'Rabbi, do have something to eat'; but he said, 'I have food to eat that you do not know about.' So the disciples said to one another, 'Has someone brought him food?'

REFRAIN FOLLOWED BY SILENCE

But Jesus said, 'My food is to do the will of the one who sent me, and to complete his work. Do you not have a saying: "Four months and then the harvest"? Well, I tell you, look around you, look at the fields; already they are white, ready for harvest!'

REFRAIN FOLLOWED BY SILENCE

'Already the reaper is being paid his wages, already he is bringing in the grain for eternal life, so that sower and reaper can rejoice together. For here the proverb holds true: one sows, another reaps; I sent you to reap a harvest you have not

18

laboured for. Others have laboured for it; and you have come into the rewards of their labour.'

REFRAIN FOLLOWED BY SILENCE

Many Samaritans in that town believed in him on the strength of the woman's words of testimony, 'He told me everything I have done.' So, when the Samaritans came up to him, they begged him to stay with them. He stayed for two days, and many more came to believe on the strength of the words he spoke to them; and they said to the woman, 'Now we believe no longer because of what you told us; we have heard him ourselves and we know that he is indeed the Saviour of the world.'

REFRAIN FOLLOWED BY SILENCE

Glory to the Father, and to the Son, and to the Holy Spirit: as it was in the beginning, is now, and shall be for ever.   Amen.

Lord, you gave your time to strangers and they responded to you. Help us to be generous in going out to the needs of others.   Amen.

ALTERNATIVE REFRAIN:
> *The Lord is loving unto every man:*
> *And his mercy is over all his works.*

Life restored

John 4:43–54

In the name of the Father, and of the Son, and of the Holy Spirit. Amen.

Our Father . . .

Jesus left for Galilee. He himself had declared that a prophet is not honoured in his own home town. On his arrival the Galileans received him well, having seen all that he had done at Jerusalem during the festival which they too had attended.

> *Blessed be Jesus, true God and true man.*
> *Blessed be the name of Jesus.*

SILENCE

He went again to Cana in Galilee, where he had changed the water into wine. And there was a court official whose son was ill at Capernaum; hearing that Jesus had arrived in Galilee from Judaea, he went and asked him to come and cure his son, as he was at the point of death.

REFRAIN FOLLOWED BY SILENCE

Jesus said to him, 'Unless you see signs and portents you will not believe!' 'Sir,' answered the official, 'come down before my child dies.' 'Go home,' said Jesus, 'your son will live.'

REFRAIN FOLLOWED BY SILENCE

The man believed what Jesus had said and went on his way home; and while he was still on the way his servants met him with the news that his boy was alive. He asked them when the boy had begun to recover. They replied, 'The fever left him yesterday at the seventh hour.' The father realised that this was exactly the time when Jesus had said, 'Your son will live'; and he and all his household believed.

REFRAIN FOLLOWED BY SILENCE

This new sign, the second, Jesus performed on his return from Judaea to Galilee.

REFRAIN FOLLOWED BY SILENCE

Glory to the Father, and to the Son, and to the Holy Spirit: as it was in the beginning, is now, and shall be for ever.   Amen.

God our Father, we press our open wounds to the precious wounds of Jesus your Son, that your will and ours may be one. Through these shared wounds, may we be healed and bring your healing love to others.   Amen.*

ALTERNATIVE REFRAIN:
> *It is he who heals the broken in heart:*
> *And binds up their wounds.*

---

* For this prayer, see Gabriel Harty OP, *Healing Light of the Rosary* (London, Veritas Publications 1983).

Lost powers restored

John 5:1–24

In the name of the Father, and of the Son, and of the Holy Spirit. Amen.

Our Father . . .

After this there was a Jewish festival, and Jesus went up to Jerusalem. Now in Jerusalem next to the Sheep Pool there is a pool called Bethesda in Hebrew, which has five porticos; and under these were crowds of sick people, blind, lame, paralysed. One man there had an illness which had lasted thirty-eight years, and when Jesus saw him lying there and knew he had been in that condition for a long time, he said, 'Do you want to be well again?' 'Sir,' replied the sick man, 'I have no one to put me into the pool when the water is disturbed; and while I am still on the way, someone else gets down there before me.' Jesus said, 'Get up, pick up your mat and walk around.' The man was cured at once, and he picked up his sleeping-mat and started to walk around.

Blessed be Jesus, true God and true man.
Blessed be the name of Jesus.

SILENCE

Now that day happened to be the Sabbath, so the Jews said to the man who had been cured, 'It is the Sabbath; you are not allowed to carry your sleeping-mat.' He replied, 'But the man who cured me told me, "Pick up your mat and walk around." ' They asked, 'Who is the man who said to you, "Pick up your mat and walk around"?' The man had no idea who it was, since Jesus had disappeared, as the place was crowded. After a while Jesus met him in the Temple and said, 'Now you are well again, do not sin any more, or something worse may happen to you.'

REFRAIN FOLLOWED BY SILENCE

The man went back and told the Jews that it was Jesus who had cured him. It was because he did things like this on the

Sabbath that the Jews began to harass Jesus. His answer to them was, 'My Father still goes on working, and I am at work, too.' But that only made the Jews even more intent on killing him, because not only was he breaking the Sabbath, but he spoke of God as his own Father and so made himself God's equal.

REFRAIN FOLLOWED BY SILENCE

To this Jesus replied, 'In all truth I tell you, by himself the Son can do nothing; he can do only what he sees the Father doing: and whatever the Father does the Son does too. For the Father loves the Son and shows him everything he himself does, and he will show him even greater things than these, works that will astonish you.'

REFRAIN FOLLOWED BY SILENCE

'Thus, as the Father raises the dead and gives them life, so the Son gives life to anyone he chooses; for the Father judges no one; he has entrusted all judgement to the Son, so that all may honour the Son as they honour the Father. Whoever refuses honour to the Son refuses honour to the Father who sent him. In all truth I tell you, whoever listens to my words, and believes in the one who sent me, has eternal life; without being brought to judgement such a person has passed from death to life.'

REFRAIN FOLLOWED BY SILENCE

Glory to the Father, and to the Son, and to the Holy Spirit: as it was in the beginning, is now, and shall be for ever.   Amen.

Lord, we place our infirmities in your hands, knowing that you alone can heal. Bring healing where you will for the salvation of our souls and bodies and for the glory of your name.   Amen.

ALTERNATIVE REFRAIN:
He who hears my words has eternal life:
He has passed from death into life.

23

The glory of the Father

John 5:25–47

In the name of the Father, and of the Son, and of the Holy Spirit. Amen.

Our Father . . .

'In all truth I tell you, the hour is coming – indeed it is already here – when the dead will hear the voice of the Son of God, and all who hear it will live. For as the Father has life in himself, so he has granted the Son also to have life in himself; and, because he is the Son of man, has granted him power to give judgement. Do not be surprised at this, for the hour is coming when the dead will leave their graves at the sound of his voice: those who did good will come forth to life; and those who did evil will come forth to judgement. By myself I can do nothing; I can judge only as I am told to judge, and my judging is just, because I seek to do not my own will but the will of him who sent me.'

> *Blessed be Jesus, true God and true man.*
> *Blessed be the name of Jesus.*

SILENCE

'Were I to testify on my own behalf, my testimony would not be true; but there is another witness who speaks on my behalf, and I know that his testimony is true. You sent messengers to John, and he gave testimony to the truth – not that I depend on human testimony; no, it is for your salvation that I mention it. John was a lamp lit and shining and for a time you were content to enjoy the light that he gave.'

REFRAIN FOLLOWED BY SILENCE

'But my testimony is greater than John's: the deeds my Father has given me to perform, these same deeds of mine testify that the Father has sent me. Besides, the Father who sent me bears witness to me himself. You have never heard his voice, you have never seen his shape, and his word finds no home in you because you do not believe in the one whom he has sent.'

REFRAIN FOLLOWED BY SILENCE

'You pore over the scriptures, believing that in them you can find eternal life; it is these scriptures that testify to me, and yet you refuse to come to me to receive life! Human glory means nothing to me. Besides, I know you too well: you have no love of God in you. I have come in the name of my Father and you refuse to accept me; if someone else should come in his own name you would accept him.'

REFRAIN FOLLOWED BY SILENCE

'How can you believe, since you look to each other for glory and are not concerned with the glory that comes from the one God? Do not imagine that I am going to accuse you before the Father: you have placed your hopes on Moses, and Moses will be the one who accuses you. If you really believed him you would believe me too, since it was about me that he was writing; but if you will not believe what he wrote, how can you believe what I say?'

REFRAIN FOLLOWED BY SILENCE

Glory to the Father, and to the Son, and to the Holy Spirit: as it was in the beginning, is now, and shall be for ever.   Amen.

Pity our weakness, Lord, and help us to look to you for praise, and not to the good opinion of others.   Amen.

ALTERNATIVE REFRAIN:
> *Let us rejoice in the Lord:*
> *With songs let us praise him.*

The feeding of the five thousand

John: 6:1–15

In the name of the Father, and of the Son, and of the Holy Spirit. Amen.

Our Father . . .

After this, Jesus crossed the sea of Galilee – or of Tiberias – and a large crowd followed him, impressed by the signs he had done in curing the sick. Jesus climbed the hillside and sat down there with his disciples. The time of the Jewish Passover was near.

> *Blessed be Jesus, true God and true man.*
> *Blessed be the name of Jesus.*

SILENCE

Looking up, Jesus saw the crowds approaching and said to Philip, 'Where can we buy some bread for these people to eat?' He said this only to put Philip to the test; he himself knew exactly what he was going to do.

REFRAIN FOLLOWED BY SILENCE

Philip answered, 'Two hundred denarii would not buy enough to give them a little piece each.' One of his disciples, Andrew, Simon Peter's brother, said, 'Here is a small boy with five barley loaves and two fish; but what is that among so many?' Jesus said to them, 'Make the people sit down.' There was plenty of grass there, and as many as five thousand men sat down.

REFRAIN FOLLOWED BY SILENCE

Then Jesus took the loaves, gave thanks, and distributed them to those who were sitting there; he then did the same with the fish, distributing as much as they wanted. When they had eaten enough he said to the disciples, 'Pick up the pieces left over, so that nothing is wasted.' So they picked them up and filled twelve large baskets with scraps left over from the meal of five barley loaves.

REFRAIN FOLLOWED BY SILENCE

Seeing the sign that he had done, the people said, 'This is indeed the prophet who is to come into the world.' Jesus, as he realised they were about to come and take him by force and make him king, fled back to the hills alone.

REFRAIN FOLLOWED BY SILENCE

Glory to the Father, and to the Son, and to the Holy Spirit: as it was in the beginning, is now, and shall be for ever.   Amen.

We thank you, Lord, that you feed us in body and soul. Give us grace that we may share with others the good things we receive.   Amen.

ALTERNATIVE REFRAIN:
The bread of God is he who comes down from heaven:
And gives life to the world.

The bread of life

John: 6:16–35

In the name of the Father, and of the Son, and of the Holy Spirit. Amen.

Our Father . . .

That evening the disciples went down to the shore of the sea and got into a boat to make for Capernaum on the other side of the sea. It was getting dark by now and Jesus had still not rejoined them. The wind was strong, and the sea was getting rough. They had rowed three or four miles when they saw Jesus walking on the sea and coming towards the boat. They were afraid, but he said, 'It's me. Don't be afraid.' They were ready to take him into the boat, and immediately it reached the shore at the place they were making for.

> *Blessed be Jesus, true God and true man.*
> *Blessed be the name of Jesus.*

SILENCE

Next day, the crowd that had stayed on the other side saw that only one boat had been there, and that Jesus had not got into the boat with his disciples, but that the disciples had set off by themselves. Other boats, however, had put in from Tiberias, near the place where the bread had been eaten. When the people saw that neither Jesus nor his disciples were there, they got into those boats and crossed to Capernaum to look for Jesus. When they found him on the other side, they said to him, 'Rabbi, when did you come here?' Jesus answered, 'In all truth I tell you, you are looking for me not because you have seen the signs but because you had all the bread you wanted to eat. Do not work for food that goes bad, but work for food that endures for eternal life, which the Son of man will give you, for on him the Father, God himself, has set his seal.'

REFRAIN FOLLOWED BY SILENCE

Then they said to him, 'What must we do if we are to carry out God's work?' Jesus gave them this answer, 'This is carrying out God's work: you must believe in the one he has sent.'

REFRAIN FOLLOWED BY SILENCE

So they said, 'What sign will you yourself do, the sight of which will make us believe in you? What work will you do? Our fathers ate manna in the desert; as scripture says: *He gave them bread from heaven to eat.*' Jesus answered them, 'In all truth I tell you, it was not Moses who gave you the bread from heaven, it is my Father who gives you the bread from heaven, the true bread; for the bread of God is the bread which comes down from heaven and gives life to the world.'

REFRAIN FOLLOWED BY SILENCE

'Sir,' they said, 'give us that bread always.' Jesus answered them, 'I am the bread of life. No one who comes to me will ever hunger; no one who believes in me will ever thirst.'

REFRAIN FOLLOWED BY SILENCE

Glory to the Father, and to the Son, and to the Holy Spirit: as it was in the beginning, is now, and shall be for ever. Amen.

Lord, make yourself known to us in the breaking of the bread. Amen.

ALTERNATIVE REFRAIN:
He who comes to me shall never hunger:
And he who believes in me shall never thirst.

Jesus the living bread

John 6:44–69

In the name of the Father, and of the Son, and of the Holy Spirit. Amen.

Our Father . . .

'No one can come to me unless drawn by the Father who sent me, and I will raise that person up on the last day. It is written in the prophets: *they will all be taught by God*; everyone who has listened to the Father, and learnt from him, comes to me. Not that anybody has seen the Father, except him who has his being from God: he has seen the Father. In all truth I tell you, everyone who believes has eternal life.'

> *Blessed be Jesus, true God and true man.*
> *Blessed be the name of Jesus.*

SILENCE

'I am the bread of life. Your fathers ate manna in the desert and they are dead; but this is the bread which comes down from heaven, so that a person may eat it and not die. I am the living bread which has come down from heaven. Anyone who eats this bread will live for ever; and the bread that I shall give is my flesh, for the life of the world.'

REFRAIN FOLLOWED BY SILENCE

Then the Jews started arguing among themselves, 'How can this man give us his flesh to eat?' Jesus replied to them, 'In all truth I tell you, if you do not eat the flesh of the Son of man and drink his blood, you have no life in you. Anyone who does eat my flesh and drink my blood has eternal life, and I shall raise that person up on the last day. For my flesh is real food and my blood is real drink. Whoever eats my flesh and drinks my blood lives in me and I live in that person. As the living Father sent me and I draw life from the Father, so whoever eats me will also draw life from me. This is the bread which has come down from heaven; it is not like the bread our ancestors ate: they are dead, but anyone who eats this bread will live for ever.'

REFRAIN FOLLOWED BY SILENCE

This is what he taught at Capernaum in the synagogue. After hearing it, many of his followers said, 'This is intolerable language. How could anyone accept it?' Jesus was aware that his followers were complaining about it and said, 'Does this disturb you? What if you should see the Son of man ascend to where he was before? It is the spirit that gives life, the flesh has nothing to offer. The words I have spoken to you are spirit and they are life. But there are some of you who do not believe.' For Jesus knew from the outset who did not believe and who was to betray him. He went on, 'This is why I told you that no one could come to me except by the gift of the Father.'

REFRAIN FOLLOWED BY SILENCE

After this, many of his disciples went away and accompanied him no more. Then Jesus said to the Twelve, 'What about you, do you want to go away too?' Simon Peter answered, 'Lord, to whom shall we go? You have the message of eternal life, and we believe; we have come to know that you are the Holy One of God.'

REFRAIN FOLLOWED BY SILENCE

Glory to the Father, and to the Son, and to the Holy Spirit: as it was in the beginning, is now, and shall be for ever.   Amen.

Lord, you are the living bread: feed us with the food of eternal life.   Amen.

ALTERNATIVE REFRAIN:
This is the bread that came down from heaven:
That a man may eat thereof and not die.

The feast of Tabernacles

John 7:2–30

In the name of the Father, and of the Son, and of the Holy Spirit. Amen.

Our Father . . .

As the Jewish feast of Shelters drew near, his brothers said to him, 'Leave this place and go to Judaea, so that your disciples, too, can see the works you are doing; no one who wants to be publicly known acts in secret; if this is what you are doing, you should reveal yourself to the world.' Not even his brothers had faith in him. Jesus answered, 'For me the right time has not come yet, but for you any time is the right time. The world cannot hate you, but it does hate me, because I give evidence that its ways are evil. Go up to the festival yourselves: I am not going to this festival, because for me the time is not ripe yet.'

> *Blessed be Jesus, true God and true man.*
> *Blessed be the name of Jesus.*

SILENCE

However, after his brothers had left for the festival, he went up as well, not publicly but secretly. At the festival the Jews were on the look-out for him: 'Where is he?' they said. There was a great deal of talk about him in the crowds. Some said, 'He is a good man'; others, 'No, he is leading the people astray.' Yet no one spoke about him openly, for fear of the Jews.

REFRAIN FOLLOWED BY SILENCE

When the festival was half over, Jesus went to the Temple and began to teach. The Jews were astonished and said, 'How did he learn to read? He has not been educated.' Jesus answered them, 'My teaching is not from myself: it comes from the one who sent me; anyone who is prepared to do his will, will know whether my teaching is from God or whether I speak on my own account. When someone speaks on his own account, he is seeking honour for himself; but when he is seeking the honour of the person who sent him, then he is true and altogether without dishonesty. Did not Moses give you the Law? And yet not one of you keeps the Law!'

REFRAIN FOLLOWED BY SILENCE

'Why do you want to kill me?' The crowd replied, 'You are mad! Who wants to kill you?' Jesus answered, 'One work I did, and you are all amazed at it. Moses ordered you to practise circumcision – not that it began with him, it goes back to the patriarchs – and you circumcise on the Sabbath. Now if someone can be circumcised on the Sabbath so that the Law of Moses is not broken, why are you angry with me for making someone completely healthy on a Sabbath? Do not keep judging according to appearances; let your judgement be according to what is right.'

REFRAIN FOLLOWED BY SILENCE

Meanwhile some of the people of Jerusalem were saying, 'Isn't this the man they want to kill? And here he is, speaking openly, and they have nothing to say to him! Can it be true the authorities have recognised that he is the Christ? Yet we all know where he comes from, but when the Christ appears no one will know where he comes from.' Then, as Jesus was teaching in the Temple, he cried out, 'You know me and you know where I came from. Yet I have not come of my own accord: but he who sent me is true. You do not know him, but I know him because I have my being from him and it was he who sent me.' They wanted to arrest him then, but because his hour had not yet come no one laid a hand on him.

REFRAIN FOLLOWED BY SILENCE

Glory to the Father, and to the Son, and to the Holy Spirit: as it was in the beginning, is now, and shall be for ever.   Amen.

Father, enable us to do your will, that we may know him whom you have sent to be our Saviour and our Lord.   Amen.

ALTERNATIVE REFRAIN:
If you keep my commandments:
You shall abide in my love.

The fountain of life

John 7:31–47

In the name of the Father, and of the Son, and of the Holy Spirit. Amen.

Our Father . . .

There were many people in the crowds, however, who believed in him; they were saying, 'When the Christ comes, will he give more signs than this man has?' Hearing that talk like this about him was spreading among the people, the Pharisees sent the Temple guards to arrest him. Then Jesus said, 'For a short time I am with you still; then I shall go back to the one who sent me. You will look for me and will not find me; where I am you cannot come.'

> *Blessed be Jesus, true God and true man.*
> *Blessed be the name of Jesus.*

SILENCE

So the Jews said to one another, 'Where is he intending to go that we shall not be able to find him? Is he intending to go abroad to the people who are dispersed among the Greeks and to teach the Greeks? What does he mean when he says: "You will look for me and will not find me; where I am you cannot come"?'

REFRAIN FOLLOWED BY SILENCE

On the last day, the great day of the festival, Jesus stood and cried out, 'Let anyone who is thirsty come to me! Let anyone who believes in me come and drink! As scripture says, "From his heart shall flow streams of living water." ' He was speaking of the Spirit which those who believed in him were to receive; for there was no Spirit as yet because Jesus had not yet been glorified.

REFRAIN FOLLOWED BY SILENCE

Some of the crowd who had been listening said, 'He is indeed the prophet,' and some said, 'He is the Christ,' but others said, 'Would the Christ come from Galilee? Does not scripture say that the Christ must be descended from David and come from Bethlehem, the village where David was?' So the people could not agree about him. Some wanted to arrest him, but no one actually laid a hand on him.

REFRAIN FOLLOWED BY SILENCE

The guards went back to the chief priests and Pharisees who said to them, 'Why haven't you brought him?' The guards replied, 'No one has ever spoken like this man.'

REFRAIN FOLLOWED BY SILENCE

Glory to the Father, and to the Son, and to the Holy Spirit: as it was in the beginning, is now, and shall be for ever.   Amen.

Lord, deepen our desire for you, who alone can fill our needs.   Amen.

ALTERNATIVE REFRAIN:
Let anyone who is thirsty come to me!:
Let anyone who believes in me come and drink!

The woman brought before Jesus

John 8:1–11

In the name of the Father, and of the Son, and of the Holy Spirit. Amen.

Our Father . . .

Jesus went to the Mount of Olives. At daybreak he appeared in the Temple again; and as all the people came to him, he sat down and began to teach them.

Blessed be Jesus, true God and true man.
Blessed be the name of Jesus.

SILENCE

The scribes and Pharisees brought a woman along who had been caught committing adultery; and making her stand there in the middle they said to Jesus, 'Master, this woman was caught in the very act of committing adultery, and in the Law Moses has ordered us to stone women of this kind. What have you got to say?'

REFRAIN FOLLOWED BY SILENCE

They asked him this as a test, looking for an accusation to use against him. But Jesus bent down and started writing on the ground with his finger. As they persisted with their question he straightened up and said, 'Let the one among you who is guiltless be the first to throw a stone at her.'

REFRAIN FOLLOWED BY SILENCE

Then he bent down and continued writing on the ground. When they heard this they went away one by one, beginning with the eldest, until the last one had gone and Jesus was left alone with the woman, who remained in the middle.

REFRAIN FOLLOWED BY SILENCE

Jesus again straightened up and said, 'Woman, where are they? Has no one condemned you?' 'No one, sir,' she replied. 'Neither do I condemn you,' said Jesus. 'Go away, and from this moment sin no more.'

REFRAIN FOLLOWED BY SILENCE

Glory to the Father, and to the Son, and to the Holy Spirit: as it was in the beginning, is now, and shall be for ever. Amen.

Lord, we pray: Strengthen those who stand; comfort and help the fainthearted; raise up the fallen; and finally beat down Satan under our feet. Amen.

ALTERNATIVE REFRAIN:
The Lord is loving unto every man:
And his mercy is over all his works.

The Light of the world

John 8:12–26

In the name of the Father, and of the Son, and of the Holy
Spirit.   Amen.

Our Father . . .

When Jesus spoke to the people again, he said, 'I am the light
of the world; anyone who follows me will not be walking in
the dark but will have the light of life.'

> *Blessed be Jesus, true God and true man.*
> *Blessed be the name of Jesus.*

SILENCE

At this the Pharisees said to him, 'You are testifying on your
own behalf; your testimony is not true.' Jesus replied, 'Even
though I am testifying on my own behalf, my testimony is
still true, because I know where I have come from and where
I am going; but you do not know where I come from or
where I am going. You judge by human standards; I judge no
one, but if I judge, my judgement will be true, because I am
not alone: the one who sent me is with me; and in your Law
it is written that the testimony of two witnesses is true. I
testify on my own behalf, but the Father who sent me testifies
on my behalf, too.'

REFRAIN FOLLOWED BY SILENCE

They asked him, 'Where is your Father then?' Jesus answered,
'You do not know me, nor do you know my Father; if you
did know me, you would know my Father as well.' He spoke
these words in the Treasury, while teaching in the Temple.
No one arrested him, because his hour had not yet come.

REFRAIN FOLLOWED BY SILENCE

Again he said to them, 'I am going away; you will look for
me and you will die in your sin. Where I am going, you
cannot come.' So the Jews said to one another, 'Is he going

to kill himself, that he says, "Where I am going, you cannot come"?' Jesus went on, 'You are from below; I am from above. You are of this world; I am not of this world. I have told you already: you will die in your sins. Yes, if you do not believe that I am He, you will die in your sins.'

REFRAIN FOLLOWED BY SILENCE

So they said to him, 'Who are you?' Jesus answered, 'What I have told you from the outset. About you I have much to say and much to judge; but the one who sent me is true, and what I declare to the world I have learnt from him.'

REFRAIN FOLLOWED BY SILENCE

Glory to the Father, and to the Son, and to the Holy Spirit: as it was in the beginning, is now, and shall be for ever.   Amen.

Lord, penetrate our inmost being with your light and truth, that our way of life may be one of faithful service to you.   Amen.

ALTERNATIVE REFRAIN:
> *Save us and help us:*
> *We humbly beseech thee, O Lord.*

The truth shall set you free

John 8:27–41

In the name of the Father, and of the Son, and of the Holy Spirit. Amen.

Our Father . . .

They did not recognise that he was talking to them about the Father. So Jesus said, 'When you have lifted up the Son of man, then you will know that I am He and that I do nothing of my own accord. What I say is what the Father has taught me; he who sent me is with me, and has not left me to myself, for I always do what pleases him.'

> *Blessed be Jesus, true God and true man.*
> *Blessed be the name of Jesus.*

SILENCE

As he was saying this, many came to believe in him. To the Jews who believed in him Jesus said, 'If you make my word your home you will indeed be my disciples; you will come to know the truth, and the truth will set you free.'

REFRAIN FOLLOWED BY SILENCE

They answered, 'We are descended from Abraham and we have never been the slaves of anyone; what do you mean, "You will be set free"?' Jesus replied, 'In all truth I tell you, everyone who commits sin is a slave. Now a slave has no permanent standing in the household, but a son belongs to it for ever. So if the Son sets you free, you will indeed be free.'

REFRAIN FOLLOWED BY SILENCE

'I know that you are descended from Abraham; but you want to kill me because my word finds no place in you. What I speak of is what I have seen at my Father's side, and you too put into action the lessons you have learnt from your father.'

REFRAIN FOLLOWED BY SILENCE

They repeated, 'Our father is Abraham.' Jesus said to them, 'If you are Abraham's children, do as Abraham did. As it is, you want to kill me, a man who has told you the truth as I have learnt it from God; that is not what Abraham did. You are doing your father's work.' They replied, 'We were not born illegitimate, the only father we have is God.'

REFRAIN FOLLOWED BY SILENCE

Glory to the Father, and to the Son, and to the Holy Spirit: as it was in the beginning, is now, and shall be for ever.   Amen.

Release us, Lord, from the bondage of selfish desires, and help us to find the freedom which lies only in you.

ALTERNATIVE REFRAIN:
> *If the Son sets you free:*
> *You will be free indeed.*

Before Abraham was, I am

John 8:42–59

In the name of the Father, and of the Son, and of the Holy Spirit. Amen.

Our Father . . .

'If God were your father, you would love me, since I have my origin in God and have come from him. I did not come of my own accord, but he sent me. Why do you not understand what I say? Because you cannot bear to listen to my words.'

> *Blessed be Jesus, true God and true man.*
> *Blessed be the name of Jesus.*

SILENCE

'You are from your father, the devil, and you prefer to do what your father wants. He was a murderer from the start; he was never grounded in the truth; there is no truth in him at all. When he lies he is speaking true to his nature, because he is a liar, and the father of lies. But it is because I speak the truth that you do not believe me. Can any of you convict me of sin? If I speak the truth, why do you not believe me? Whoever comes from God listens to the words of God; the reason why you do not listen is that you are not from God.'

REFRAIN FOLLOWED BY SILENCE

The Jews replied, 'Are we not right in saying that you are a Samaritan and possessed by a devil?' Jesus answered, 'I am not possessed; but I honour my Father, and you deny me honour. I do not seek my own glory; there is someone who does seek it and is the judge of it. In all truth I tell you, whoever keeps my word will never see death.'

REFRAIN FOLLOWED BY SILENCE

The Jews said, 'Now we know that you are possessed. Abraham is dead, and the prophets are dead, and yet you say,

"Whoever keeps my word will never know the taste of death."
Are you greater than our father Abraham, who is dead? The
prophets are dead too. Who are you claiming to be?' Jesus
answered, 'If I were to seek my own glory, my glory would
be worth nothing. In fact, my glory is conferred by the Father,
by the one of whom you say, "He is our God," although you
do not know him. But I know him, and if I were to say,
"I do not know him," I should be a liar, as you yourselves
are. But I do know him, and I keep his word.'

REFRAIN FOLLOWED BY SILENCE

'Your father Abraham rejoiced to think that he would see my
Day; he saw it and was glad.' The Jews then said, 'You are
not fifty yet, and you have seen Abraham!' Jesus replied, 'In
all truth I tell you, before Abraham ever was, I am.' At this
they picked up stones to throw at him; but Jesus hid himself
and left the Temple.

REFRAIN FOLLOWED BY SILENCE

Glory to the Father, and to the Son, and to the Holy Spirit: as
it was in the beginning, is now, and shall be for ever.   Amen.

From all evil and mischief, from sin, from the crafts and assaults
of the devil, good Lord, deliver us.

ALTERNATIVE REFRAIN:
> *If anyone keeps my word:*
> *He will never see death.*

The healing of the man born blind

John 9:1–17

In the name of the Father, and of the Son, and of the Holy Spirit. Amen.

Our Father . . .

As he went along, he saw a man who had been blind from birth. His disciples asked him, 'Rabbi, who sinned, this man or his parents, that he should have been born blind?' 'Neither he nor his parents sinned,' Jesus answered, 'he was born blind so that the works of God might be revealed in him.'

> *Blessed be Jesus, true God and true man.*
> *Blessed be the name of Jesus.*

SILENCE

'As long as day lasts we must carry out the work of the one who sent me; the night will soon be here when no one can work. As long as I am in the world I am the light of the world.'

REFRAIN FOLLOWED BY SILENCE

Having said this, he spat on the ground, made a paste with the spittle, put this over the eyes of the blind man, and said to him, 'Go and wash in the Pool of Siloam' (the name means 'one who has been sent'). So he went off and washed and came back able to see.

REFRAIN FOLLOWED BY SILENCE

His neighbours and the people who used to see him before (for he was a beggar) said, 'Isn't this the man who used to sit and beg?' Some said, 'Yes, it is the same one.' Others said, 'No, but he looks just like him.' The man himself said, 'Yes, I am the one.' So they said to him, 'Then how is it that your eyes were opened?' He answered, 'The man called Jesus made a paste, daubed my eyes with it and said to me, "Go off and

44

wash at Siloam"; so I went, and when I washed I gained my sight.' They asked, 'Where is he?' He answered, 'I don't know.'

REFRAIN FOLLOWED BY SILENCE

They brought to the Pharisees the man who had been blind. It had been a Sabbath day when Jesus made the paste and opened the man's eyes, so when the Pharisees asked him how he had gained his sight, he said, 'He put a paste on my eyes, and I washed, and I can see.' Then some of the Pharisees said, 'That man cannot be from God: he does not keep the Sabbath.' Others said, 'How can a sinner produce signs like this?' And there was division among them. So they spoke to the blind man again, 'What have you to say about him yourself, now that he has opened your eyes?' The man answered, 'He is a prophet.'

REFRAIN FOLLOWED BY SILENCE

Glory to the Father, and to the Son, and to the Holy Spirit: as it was in the beginning, is now, and shall be for ever.   Amen.

Lord, open our eyes that we may see.   Amen.

ALTERNATIVE REFRAIN:
O send out thy light and thy truth that they may lead me:
And bring me to thy holy hill and to thy dwelling.

If you were blind, then you would see

John 9:18–41

In the name of the Father, and of the Son, and of the Holy Spirit. Amen.

Our Father . . .

However, the Jews would not believe that the man had been blind without first sending for the parents of the man who had gained his sight and asking them, 'Is this man really the son of yours who you say was born blind? If so, how is it that he is now able to see?' His parents answered, 'We know he is our son and we know he was born blind, but how he can see, we don't know, nor who opened his eyes. Ask him. He is old enough: let him speak for himself.' His parents spoke like this out of fear of the Jews, who had already agreed to ban from the synagogue anyone who should acknowledge Jesus as the Christ. This was why his parents said, 'He is old enough: ask him.'

> *Blessed be Jesus, true God and true man.*
> *Blessed be the name of Jesus.*

SILENCE

So the Jews sent for the man again and said to him, 'Give glory to God! We are satisfied that this man is a sinner.' The man answered, 'Whether he is a sinner I don't know; all I know is that I was blind and now I can see.' They said to him, 'What did he do to you? How did he open your eyes?' He replied, 'I have told you once and you wouldn't listen. Why do you want to hear it all again? Do you want to become his disciples yourselves?'

REFRAIN FOLLOWED BY SILENCE

At this they hurled abuse at him, 'It is you who are his disciple, we are the disciples of Moses: we know that God spoke to Moses, but as for this man, we don't know where he comes from.' The man replied, 'That is just what is so amazing! You don't know where he comes from and he has opened my eyes!

We know that God doesn't listen to sinners, but God does listen to men who are devout and do his will. Ever since the world began it is unheard of for anyone to open the eyes of a man who was born blind; if this man were not from God, he wouldn't have been able to do anything.'

REFRAIN FOLLOWED BY SILENCE

They retorted, 'Are you trying to teach us, and you a sinner through and through ever since you were born!' And they ejected him.

REFRAIN FOLLOWED BY SILENCE

Jesus heard they had ejected him, and when he found him he said to him, 'Do you believe in the Son of man?' 'Sir,' the man replied, 'tell me who he is so that I may believe in him.' Jesus said, 'You have seen him; he is speaking to you.' The man said, 'Lord, I believe,' and worshipped him. Jesus said, 'It is for judgement that I have come into this world, so that those without sight may see and those with sight may become blind.' Hearing this, some Pharisees who were present said to him, 'So we are blind, are we?' Jesus replied, 'If you were blind, you would not be guilty, but since you say, "We can see," your guilt remains.

REFRAIN FOLLOWED BY SILENCE

Glory to the Father, and to the Son, and to the Holy Spirit: as it was in the beginning, is now, and shall be for ever.   Amen.

Lord, reveal to us our blindness, that being brought to a right knowledge of ourselves, we may truly see.   Amen.

ALTERNATIVE REFRAIN:
> *Lord Jesus Christ:*
> *Have mercy upon us.*

The good shepherd

John 10:1–21

In the name of the Father, and of the Son, and of the Holy Spirit. Amen.

Our Father . . .

'In all truth I tell you, anyone who does not enter the sheepfold through the gate, but climbs in some other way, is a thief and a bandit. He who enters through the gate is the shepherd of the flock; the gatekeeper lets him in, the sheep hear his voice, one by one he calls his own sheep and leads them out. When he has brought out all those that are his, he goes ahead of them, and the sheep follow because they know his voice. They will never follow a stranger, but will run away from him because they do not recognise the voice of strangers.' Jesus told them this parable but they failed to understand what he was saying to them.

> *Blessed be Jesus, true God and true man.*
> *Blessed be the name of Jesus.*

SILENCE

So Jesus spoke to them again, 'In all truth I tell you, I am the gate of the sheepfold. All who have come before me are thieves and bandits, but the sheep took no notice of them. I am the gate. Anyone who enters through me will be safe: such a one will go in and out and will find pasture. The thief comes only to steal and kill and destroy. I have come so that they may have life and have it to the full.'

REFRAIN FOLLOWED BY SILENCE

'I am the good shepherd: the good shepherd lays down his life for his sheep. The hired man, since he is not the shepherd and the sheep do not belong to him, abandons the sheep as soon as he sees a wolf coming, and runs away, and then the wolf attacks and scatters the sheep; he runs away because he is only a hired man and has no concern for the sheep.'

REFRAIN FOLLOWED BY SILENCE

'I am the good shepherd; I know my own and my own know me, just as the Father knows me and I know the Father; and I lay down my life for my sheep. And there are other sheep I have that are not of this fold, and I must lead these too. They too will listen to my voice, and there will be only one flock, one shepherd.'

REFRAIN FOLLOWED BY SILENCE

'The Father loves me, because I lay down my life in order to take it up again. No one takes it from me; I lay it down of my own free will, and as I have power to lay it down, so I have power to take it up again; and this is the command I have received from my Father.' These words caused a fresh division among the Jews. Many said, 'He is possessed, he is raving; why do you listen to him?' Others said, 'These are not the words of a man possessed by a devil: could a devil open the eyes of the blind?'

REFRAIN FOLLOWED BY SILENCE

Glory to the Father, and to the Son, and to the Holy Spirit: as it was in the beginning, is now, and shall be for ever.   Amen.

You, Lord, are the good shepherd. We pray that you will guide us into all truth and that you will restore us when we stray.   Amen.

ALTERNATIVE REFRAIN:
The Lord himself is your keeper:
The Lord is your defence upon your right hand.

The Father and I are one

John 10:22–42

In the name of the Father, and of the Son, and of the Holy Spirit. Amen.

Our Father . . .

It was the time of the feast of Dedication in Jerusalem. It was winter, and Jesus was in the Temple walking up and down in the Portico of Solomon. The Jews gathered round him and said, 'How much longer are you going to keep us in suspense? If you are the Christ, tell us openly.'

> *Blessed be Jesus, true God and true man.*
> *Blessed be the name of Jesus.*

SILENCE

Jesus replied, 'I have told you, but you do not believe. The works I do in my Father's name are my witness; but you do not believe, because you are no sheep of mine. The sheep that belong to me listen to my voice; I know them and they follow me. I give them eternal life; they will never be lost and no one will ever steal them from my hand. The Father, for what he has given me, is greater than anyone, and no one can steal anything from the Father's hand. The Father and I are one.'

REFRAIN FOLLOWED BY SILENCE

The Jews fetched stones to stone him, so Jesus said to them, 'I have shown you many good works from my Father; for which of these are you stoning me?' The Jews answered him, 'We are stoning you, not for doing a good work, but for blasphemy; though you are only a man, you claim to be God.'

REFRAIN FOLLOWED BY SILENCE

Jesus answered, 'Is it not written in your Law: *I said, you are gods*? So it uses the word "gods" of those people to whom the word of God was addressed – and scripture cannot be set aside.

Yet to someone whom the Father has consecrated and sent into the world you say, "You are blaspheming," because I said, "I am Son of God." '

REFRAIN FOLLOWED BY SILENCE

'If I am not doing my Father's work, there is no need to believe me; but if I am doing it, then even if you refuse to believe in me, at least believe in the work I do; then you will know for certain that the Father is in me and I am in the Father.' They again wanted to arrest him then, but he eluded their clutches. He went back again to the far side of the Jordan to the district where John had been baptising at first and he stayed there. Many people who came to him said, 'John gave no signs, but all he said about this man was true'; and many of them believed in him.

REFRAIN FOLLOWED BY SILENCE

Glory to the Father, and to the Son, and to the Holy Spirit: as it was in the beginning, is now, and shall be for ever.   Amen.

Lord, we believe that you are the Christ, the Son of God. We pray that what we believe in our hearts may be revealed in our lives.   Amen.

ALTERNATIVE REFRAIN:
O Lord, in you have I trusted:
Let me never be confounded.

The one whom you love is sick

John 11:1–27

In the name of the Father, and of the Son, and of the Holy Spirit. Amen.

Our Father . . .

There was a man named Lazarus of Bethany, the village of Mary and her sister, Martha, and he was ill. It was the same Mary, the sister of the sick man Lazarus, who anointed the Lord with ointment and wiped his feet with her hair. The sisters sent this message to Jesus, 'Lord, the man you love is ill.' On receiving the message, Jesus said, 'This sickness will not end in death, but it is for God's glory so that through it the Son of God may be glorified.'

> *Blessed be Jesus, true God and true man.*
> *Blessed be the name of Jesus.*

SILENCE

Jesus loved Martha and her sister and Lazarus, yet when he heard that he was ill he stayed where he was for two more days before saying to the disciples, 'Let us go back to Judaea.' The disciples said, 'Rabbi, it is not long since the Jews were trying to stone you; are you going back there again?' Jesus replied, 'Are there not twelve hours in the day? No one who walks in the daytime stumbles, having the light of this world to see by; anyone who walks around at night stumbles, having no light as a guide.'

REFRAIN FOLLOWED BY SILENCE

He said that and then added, 'Our friend Lazarus is at rest; I am going to wake him.' The disciples said to him, 'Lord, if he is at rest he will be saved.' Jesus was speaking of the death of Lazarus, but they thought that by 'rest' he meant 'sleep'; so Jesus put it plainly, 'Lazarus is dead; and for your sake I am glad I was not there because now you will believe. But let us go to him.' Then Thomas – known as the Twin – said to the other disciples, 'Let us go to die with him.'

REFRAIN FOLLOWED BY SILENCE

On arriving, Jesus found that Lazarus had been in the tomb for four days already. Bethany is only about two miles from Jerusalem, and many Jews had come to Martha and Mary to comfort them about their brother. When Martha heard that Jesus was coming she went to meet him. Mary remained sitting in the house. Martha said to Jesus, 'Lord, if you had been here, my brother would not have died, but even now I know that God will grant whatever you ask of him.' Jesus said to her, 'Your brother will rise again.'

REFRAIN FOLLOWED BY SILENCE

Martha said, 'I know he will rise again at the resurrection on the last day.' Jesus said, 'I am the resurrection. Anyone who believes in me, even though that person dies, will live, and whoever lives and believes in me will never die. Do you believe this?' 'Yes, Lord,' she said, 'I believe that you are the Christ, the Son of God, the one who was to come into this world.'

REFRAIN FOLLOWED BY SILENCE

Glory to the Father, and to the Son, and to the Holy Spirit: as it was in the beginning, is now, and shall be for ever.   Amen.

Choose, Lord, the time of your coming, that the glory of God may be revealed.   Amen.

ALTERNATIVE REFRAIN:
I am the resurrection and the life:
Whoever lives and believes in me shall never die.

Lazarus is raised

John 11:28–46, 53–54

In the name of the Father, and of the Son, and of the Holy Spirit. Amen.

Our Father . . .

When (Martha) had said this, she went and called her sister Mary, saying in a low voice, 'The Master is here and wants to see you.' Hearing this, Mary got up quickly and went to him. Jesus had not yet come into the village; he was still at the place where Martha had met him. When the Jews who were in the house comforting Mary saw her get up so quickly and go out, they followed her, thinking that she was going to the tomb to weep there.

> *Blessed be Jesus, true God and true man.*
> *Blessed be the name of Jesus.*

SILENCE

Mary went to Jesus, and as soon as she saw him she threw herself at his feet, saying, 'Lord, if you had been here, my brother would not have died.' At the sight of her tears, and those of the Jews who had come with her, Jesus was greatly distressed, and with a profound sigh he said, 'Where have you put him?' They said, 'Lord, come and see.'

REFRAIN FOLLOWED BY SILENCE

Jesus wept; and the Jews said, 'See how much he loved him!' But there were some who remarked, 'He opened the eyes of the blind man. Could he not have prevented this man's death?' Sighing again, Jesus reached the tomb: it was a cave with a stone to close the opening. Jesus said, 'Take the stone away.' Martha, the dead man's sister, said to him, 'Lord, by now he will smell; this is the fourth day since he died.' Jesus replied, 'Have I not told you that if you believe, you will see the glory of God?' So they took the stone away.

REFRAIN FOLLOWED BY SILENCE

Then Jesus lifted up his eyes and said: 'Father, I thank you for hearing my prayer. I myself knew that you hear me always, but I speak for the sake of all these who are standing around me, so that they may believe it was you who sent me.' When he had said this, he cried with a loud voice, 'Lazarus, come out!' The dead man came out, his feet and hands bound with strips of material, and a cloth over his face. Jesus said to them, 'Unbind him, let him go free.'

REFRAIN FOLLOWED BY SILENCE

Many of the Jews who had come to visit Mary, and had seen what he did, believed in him, but some of them went to the Pharisees to tell them what Jesus had done . . . From that day onwards they were determined to kill him. So Jesus no longer went about openly among the Jews, but left the district for a town called Ephraim, in the country bordering on the desert, and stayed there with his disciples.

REFRAIN FOLLOWED BY SILENCE

Glory to the Father, and to the Son, and to the Holy Spirit: as it was in the beginning, is now, and shall be for ever.   Amen.

Lord, you spoke to Lazarus and he came out from the tomb. Enable us to hear your voice calling us to enrichment of life and to the loosening of those things which do bind us.   Amen.

ALTERNATIVE REFRAIN:
My soul proclaims the greatness of the Lord:
And my spirit rejoices in God my Saviour.

The anointing at Bethany

John: 12:1–11

In the name of the Father, and of the Son, and of the Holy Spirit. Amen.

Our Father . . .

Six days before the Passover, Jesus went to Bethany, where Lazarus was, whom he had raised from the dead. They gave a dinner for him there; Martha waited on them and Lazarus was among those at table.

> *Blessed be Jesus, true God and true man.*
> *Blessed be the name of Jesus.*

SILENCE

Mary brought in a pound of very costly ointment, pure nard, and with it anointed the feet of Jesus, wiping them with her hair; the house was filled with the scent of the ointment.

REFRAIN FOLLOWED BY SILENCE

Then Judas Iscariot – one of his disciples, the man who was to betray him – said, 'Why was this ointment not sold for three hundred denarii and the money given to the poor?' He said this, not because he cared about the poor, but because he was a thief; he was in charge of the common fund and used to help himself to the contents.

REFRAIN FOLLOWED BY SILENCE

So Jesus said, 'Leave her alone; let her keep it for the day of my burial. You have the poor with you always, you will not always have me.'

REFRAIN FOLLOWED BY SILENCE

Meanwhile a large number of Jews heard that he was there and came not only on account of Jesus but also to see Lazarus whom he had raised from the dead. Then the chief priests decided to kill Lazarus as well, since it was on his account that many of the Jews were leaving them and believing in Jesus.

REFRAIN FOLLOWED BY SILENCE

Glory to the Father, and to the Son, and to the Holy Spirit: as it was in the beginning, is now, and shall be for ever.　Amen.

We pray, Lord, that you who were glad to be anointed by Mary will pour your blessing on all sick and dying people to be anointed today.　Amen.

ALTERNATIVE REFRAIN:
> *Your love is more fragrant than wine:*
> *Your name is like ointment poured forth.**

---

* Song of Songs 1:2, 3.

Christic is glorified

John 12:12–36

In the name of the Father, and of the Son, and of the Holy Spirit. Amen.

Our Father . . .

The next day the great crowd of people who had come up for the festival heard that Jesus was on his way to Jerusalem. They took branches of palm and went out to receive him, shouting, '*Hosanna! Blessed is he who is coming in the name of the Lord*, the king of Israel.' Jesus found a young donkey and mounted it – as scripture says, '*Do not be afraid, daughter of Zion, look, your king is approaching, riding on the foal of a donkey.*' At first his disciples did not understand this, but later, after Jesus had been glorified, they remembered that this had been written about him and that this was what had happened to him.

> *Blessed be Jesus, true God and true man.*
> *Blessed be the name of Jesus.*

SILENCE

The crowd who had been with him when he called Lazarus out of the tomb and raised him from the dead kept bearing witness to it; this was another reason why the crowd came out to receive him: they had heard that he had given this sign. Then the Pharisees said to one another, 'You see, you are making no progress; look, the whole world has gone after him!'

REFRAIN FOLLOWED BY SILENCE

Among those who went up to worship at the festival were some Greeks. These approached Philip, who came from Bethsaida in Galilee, and put this request to him, 'Sir, we should like to see Jesus.' Philip went to tell Andrew, and Andrew and Philip together went to tell Jesus. Jesus replied to them, 'Now the hour has come for the Son of man to be glorified. In all truth I tell you, unless a wheat grain falls into the earth and dies, it remains only a single grain; but if it dies it yields a rich harvest. Anyone who loves his life loses it; anyone who hates his life in this world will keep it for eternal life.'

REFRAIN FOLLOWED BY SILENCE

'Whoever serves me, must follow me, and my servant will be with me wherever I am. If anyone serves me, my Father will honour him. Now my soul is troubled. What shall I say: Father, save me from this hour? But it is for this very reason that I have come to this hour. Father, glorify your name!' A voice came from heaven, 'I have glorified it, and I will again glorify it.' The crowd standing by, who heard this, said it was a clap of thunder; others said, 'It was an angel speaking to him.' Jesus answered, 'It was not for my sake that this voice came, but for yours. Now sentence is being passed on this world; now the prince of this world is to be driven out. And when I am lifted up from the earth, I shall draw all people to myself.'

REFRAIN FOLLOWED BY SILENCE

By these words he indicated the kind of death he would die. The crowd answered, 'The Law has taught us that the Christ will remain for ever. So how can you say, "The Son of man must be lifted up"? Who is this Son of man?' Jesus then said, 'The light will be with you only a little longer now. Go on your way while you have the light, or darkness will overtake you, and nobody who walks in the dark knows where he is going. While you still have the light, believe in the light so that you may become children of light.' Having said this, Jesus left them and was hidden from their sight.

REFRAIN FOLLOWED BY SILENCE

Glory to the Father, and to the Son, and to the Holy Spirit: as it was in the beginning, is now, and shall be for ever.   Amen.

Drive far from us, Lord, the snares of the enemy, and ever set to guard us the Angel of light.   Amen.

ALTERNATIVE REFRAIN:
> *Christ is the true light:*
> *Who lights everyone coming into the world.*

Witnessing to the truth

John: 12:37, 42–50

In the name of the Father, and of the Son, and of the Holy Spirit. Amen.

Our Father . . .

Though they had been present when he gave so many signs, they did not believe in him . . . And yet there were many who did believe in him, even among the leading men, but they did not admit it, because of the Pharisees and for fear of being banned from the synagogue: they put human glory before God's glory.

> *Blessed be Jesus, true God and true man.*
> *Blessed be the name of Jesus.*

SILENCE

Jesus declared publicly, 'Whoever believes in me believes not in me but in the one who sent me, and whoever sees me, sees the one who sent me.'

REFRAIN FOLLOWED BY SILENCE

'I have come into the world as light, to prevent anyone who believes in me from staying in the dark any more.'

REFRAIN FOLLOWED BY SILENCE

'If anyone hears my words and does not keep them faithfully, it is not I who shall judge such a person, since I have come not to judge the world, but to save the world: anyone who rejects me and refuses my words has his judge already: the word itself that I have spoken will be his judge on the last day.'

REFRAIN FOLLOWED BY SILENCE

'For I have not spoken of my own accord; but the Father who sent me commanded me what to say and what to speak, and

I know that his commands mean eternal life. And therefore what the Father has told me is what I speak.'

REFRAIN FOLLOWED BY SILENCE

Glory to the Father, and to the Son, and to the Holy Spirit: as it was in the beginning, is now, and shall be for ever.   Amen.

Lord, you are the light of the world, strengthen us that we may confess you in what we say and do.   Amen.

ALTERNATIVE REFRAIN:
> *Your word is a lantern to my feet:*
> *And a light to my path.*

The lowliness of love

John 13:1–17

In the name of the Father, and of the Son, and of the Holy Spirit. Amen.

Our Father . . .

Before the festival of the Passover, Jesus, knowing that his hour had come to pass from this world to the Father, having loved those who were his in the world, loved them to the end.

> *Blessed be Jesus, true God and true man.*
> *Blessed be the name of Jesus.*

SILENCE

They were at supper, and the devil had already put it into the mind of Judas Iscariot son of Simon, to betray him. Jesus knew that the Father had put everything into his hands, and that he had come from God and was returning to God, and he got up from table, removed his outer garments and, taking a towel, wrapped it round his waist; he then poured water into a basin and began to wash the disciples' feet and to wipe them with the towel he was wearing.

REFRAIN FOLLOWED BY SILENCE

He came to Simon Peter, who said to him, 'Lord, are you going to wash my feet?' Jesus answered, 'At the moment you do not know what I am doing, but later you will understand.' 'Never!' said Peter. 'You shall never wash my feet.' Jesus replied, 'If I do not wash you, you can have no share with me.' Simon Peter said, 'Well then, Lord, not only my feet, but my hands and my head as well!' Jesus said, 'No one who has had a bath needs washing, such a person is clean all over. You too are clean, though not all of you are.' He knew who was going to betray him, and that was why he said, 'though not all of you are'.

REFRAIN FOLLOWED BY SILENCE

When he had washed their feet and put on his outer garments again he went back to the table. 'Do you understand', he said, 'what I have done to you? You call me Master and Lord, and rightly; so I am. If I, then, the Lord and Master, have washed your feet, you must wash each other's feet. I have given you an example so that you may copy what I have done to you.'

REFRAIN FOLLOWED BY SILENCE

'In all truth I tell you, no servant is greater than his master, no messenger is greater than the one who sent him. Now that you know this, blessed are you if you behave accordingly.'

REFRAIN FOLLOWED BY SILENCE

Glory to the Father, and to the Son, and to the Holy Spirit: as it was in the beginning, is now, and shall be for ever.   Amen.

Grant, Lord, that we may serve one another as you have served us, in humility and gladness of heart.   Amen.

ALTERNATIVE REFRAIN:
> *Many waters cannot quench love:*
> *Neither can the floods drown it.*

And it was night

John 13:18–38

In the name of the Father, and of the Son, and of the Holy Spirit. Amen.

Our Father . . .

'I am not speaking about all of you: I know the ones I have chosen; but what scripture says must be fulfilled: "*He who shares my table takes advantage of me.*" I tell you this now, before it happens, so that when it does happen you may believe that I am He. In all truth I tell you, whoever welcomes the one I send, welcomes me, and whoever welcomes me, welcomes the one who sent me.'

> *Blessed be Jesus, true God and true man.*
> *Blessed be the name of Jesus.*

SILENCE

Having said this, Jesus was deeply disturbed and declared, 'In all truth I tell you, one of you is going to betray me.' The disciples looked at each other, wondering whom he meant. The disciple Jesus loved was reclining next to Jesus; Simon Peter signed to him and said, 'Ask who it is he means,' so leaning back close to Jesus' chest he said, 'Who is it, Lord?' Jesus answered, 'It is the one to whom I give the piece of bread that I dip in the dish.' And when he had dipped the piece of bread he gave it to Judas son of Simon Iscariot. At that instant, after Judas had taken the bread, Satan entered him. Jesus then said, 'What you are going to do, do quickly.' None of the others at table understood why he said this. Since Judas had charge of the common fund, some of them thought Jesus was telling him, 'Buy what we need for the festival,' or telling him to give something to the poor. As soon as Judas had taken the piece of bread he went out. It was night.

REFRAIN FOLLOWED BY SILENCE

When he had gone, Jesus said, 'Now has the Son of man been glorified, and in him God has been glorified. If God has been glorified in him, God will in turn glorify him in himself, and will glorify him very soon.'

REFRAIN FOLLOWED BY SILENCE

'Little children, I shall be with you only a little longer. You will look for me, and, as I told the Jews, where I am going, you cannot come. I give you a new commandment: love one another; you must love one another just as I have loved you. It is by your love for one another, that everyone will recognise you as my disciples.'

REFRAIN FOLLOWED BY SILENCE

Simon Peter said, 'Lord, where are you going?' Jesus replied, 'Now you cannot follow me where I am going, but later you shall follow me.' Peter said to him, 'Why can I not follow you now? I will lay down my life for you.' 'Lay down your life for me?' answered Jesus. 'In all truth I tell you, before the cock crows you will have disowned me three times.'

REFRAIN FOLLOWED BY SILENCE

Glory to the Father, and to the Son, and to the Holy Spirit: as it was in the beginning, is now, and shall be for ever. Amen.

O thou, who knowest the desires of our hearts and the weakness of our wills: in the hour of trial save us and help us, we humbly beseech thee, O Lord.

ALTERNATIVE REFRAIN:
You must love one another:
As I have loved you.

I am the Way, the Truth and the Life

John 14:1–10

In the name of the Father, and of the Son, and of the Holy Spirit. Amen.

Our Father . . .

'Do not let your hearts be troubled. You trust in God, trust also in me.'

> *Blessed be Jesus, true God and true man.*
> *Blessed be the name of Jesus.*

SILENCE

'In my Father's house there are many places to live in; otherwise I would have told you. I am going now to prepare a place for you, and after I have gone and prepared you a place, I shall return to take you to myself, so that you may be with me where I am. You know the way to the place where I am going.'

REFRAIN FOLLOWED BY SILENCE

Thomas said, 'Lord, we do not know where you are going, so how can we know the way?' Jesus said, 'I am the Way; I am Truth and Life. No one can come to the Father except through me. If you know me, you will know my Father too. From this moment you know him and have seen him.'

REFRAIN FOLLOWED BY SILENCE

Philip said, 'Lord, show us the Father and then we shall be satisfied.' Jesus said to him, 'Have I been with you all this time, Philip, and you still do not know me? Anyone who has seen me has seen the Father, so how can you say, "Show us the Father"? Do you not believe that I am in the Father and the Father is in me?'

REFRAIN FOLLOWED BY SILENCE

'What I say to you I do not speak of my own accord: it is the Father, living in me, who is doing his works.'

REFRAIN FOLLOWED BY SILENCE

Glory to the Father, and to the Son, and to the Holy Spirit: as it was in the beginning, is now, and shall be for ever.   Amen.

Come, Lord, that we may not stray from you who are the Way; that we may not distrust your promises, who are the Truth; and that we may not rest in anything other than you who are the Life.   Amen.

ALTERNATIVE REFRAIN:
I am the Way, the Truth and the Life:
No one comes to the Father, but by me.

A peace which the world cannot give

John 14:11–31

In the name of the Father, and of the Son, and of the Holy Spirit. Amen.

Our Father . . .

'You must believe me when I say that I am in the Father and the Father is in me; or at least believe it on the evidence of these works. In all truth I tell you, whoever believes in me will perform the same works as I do myself, and will perform even greater works, because I am going to the Father.'

> *Blessed be Jesus, true God and true man.*
> *Blessed be the name of Jesus.*

SILENCE

'Whatever you ask in my name I will do, so that the Father may be glorified in the Son. If you ask me for anything in my name, I will do it. If you love me you will keep my commandments. I shall ask the Father, and he will give you another Paraclete to be with you for ever, the Spirit of truth whom the world can never accept since it neither sees nor knows him; but you know him, because he is with you, he is in you.'

REFRAIN FOLLOWED BY SILENCE

'I shall not leave you orphans; I shall come to you. In a short time the world will no longer see me; but you will see that I live and you also will live. On that day you will know that I am in my Father and you in me and I in you. Whoever holds to my commandments and keeps them is the one who loves me; and whoever loves me will be loved by my Father, and I shall love him and reveal myself to him.'

REFRAIN FOLLOWED BY SILENCE

Judas – not Judas Iscariot – said to him, 'Lord, what has happened, that you intend to show yourself to us and not to the world?' Jesus replied, 'Anyone who loves me will keep my word, and my Father will love him, and we shall come to him and make a home in him. Anyone who does not love me does not keep my words. And the word that you hear is not my own: it is the word of the Father who sent me. I have said these things to you while still with you; but the Paraclete, the Holy Spirit, whom the Father will send in my name, will teach you everything and remind you of all I have said to you.'

REFRAIN FOLLOWED BY SILENCE

'Peace I bequeath to you, my own peace I give you, a peace which the world cannot give, this is my gift to you. Do not let your hearts be troubled or afraid. You heard me say: I am going away and shall return. If you loved me you would be glad that I am going to the Father, for the Father is greater than I. I have told you this now, before it happens, so that when it does happen, you may believe. I shall not talk to you much longer, because the prince of this world is on his way. He has no power over me, but the world must recognise that I love the Father and that I act just as the Father commanded. Come now, let us go.'

REFRAIN FOLLOWED BY SILENCE

Glory to the Father, and to the Son, and to the Holy Spirit: as it was in the beginning, is now, and shall be for ever.   Amen.

We pray, Lord, that you will give peace in our hearts, peace in our dwellings, peace in your Church, and peace among nations.   Amen.

ALTERNATIVE REFRAIN:
Peace I leave with you, my peace I give unto you:
Let not your heart be troubled, neither let it be afraid.

The true vine

John 15:1–8

In the name of the Father, and of the Son, and of the Holy Spirit. Amen.

Our Father . . .

'I am the true vine, and my father is the vinedresser. Every branch in me that bears no fruit he cuts away, and every branch that does bear fruit he prunes to make it bear even more. You are clean already, by means of the word that I have spoken to you.'

> *Blessed be Jesus, true God and true man.*
> *Blessed be the name of Jesus.*

SILENCE

'Remain in me, as I in you. As a branch cannot bear fruit all by itself, unless it remains part of the vine, neither can you unless you remain in me.'

REFRAIN FOLLOWED BY SILENCE

'I am the vine, you are the branches. Whoever remains in me, with me in him, bears fruit in plenty; for cut off from me you can do nothing.'

REFRAIN FOLLOWED BY SILENCE

'Anyone who does not remain in me is thrown away like a branch – and withers; these branches are collected and thrown on the fire and are burnt.'

REFRAIN FOLLOWED BY SILENCE

'If you remain in me and my words remain in you, you may ask for whatever you please and you will get it. It is to the glory of my Father that you should bear much fruit and be my disciples.'

REFRAIN FOLLOWED BY SILENCE

Glory to the Father, and to the Son, and to the Holy Spirit: as it was in the beginning, is now, and shall be for ever. Amen.

Lord Jesus, you have declared yourself to be the true vine giving life to your people. We pray that you will live in our hearts, and unite us to yourself and to all who live in you. Amen.

ALTERNATIVE REFRAIN:
> *Herein is my Father glorified:*
> *That you should bear much fruit.*

You are my friends

John 15:9–27

In the name of the Father, and of the Son, and of the Holy Spirit. Amen.

Our Father . . .

'I have loved you just as the Father has loved me. Remain in my love. If you keep my commandments you will remain in my love, just as I have kept my Father's commandments and remain in his love. I have told you this so that my own joy may be in you and your joy be complete. This is my commandment: love one another, as I have loved you.'

> *Blessed be Jesus, true God and true man:*
> *Blessed be the name of Jesus.*

SILENCE

'No one can have greater love than to lay down his life for his friends. You are my friends, if you do what I command you. I shall no longer call you servants, because a servant does not know his master's business; I call you friends, because I have made known to you everything I have learnt from my Father. You did not choose me, no, I chose you; and I commissioned you to go out and to bear fruit, fruit that will last; so that the Father will give you anything that you ask him in my name. My command to you is to love one another.'

REFRAIN FOLLOWED BY SILENCE

'If the world hates you, you must realise that it hated me before it hated you. If you belonged to the world, the world would love you as its own; but because you do not belong to the world, because my choice of you has drawn you out of the world, that is why the world hates you.'

REFRAIN FOLLOWED BY SILENCE

'Remember the words I said to you: a servant is not greater than his master. If they persecuted me, they will persecute you too; if they kept my word, they will keep yours as well. But it will be on my account that they will do all this to you, because they do not know the one who sent me. If I had not come, if I had not spoken to them, they would have been blameless; but as it is, they have no excuse for their sin.'

REFRAIN FOLLOWED BY SILENCE

'Anyone who hates me hates my Father. If I had not performed such works among them as no one else has ever done, they would be blameless; but as it is, in spite of what they have seen, they hate both me and my Father. But all this was only to fulfil the words written in their Law: *They hated me without reason*. When the Paraclete comes, the Spirit of truth who issues from the Father, whom I shall send to you from the Father, he will be my witness. And you too will be witnesses, because you have been with me from the beginning.'

REFRAIN FOLLOWED BY SILENCE

Glory to the Father, and to the Son, and to the Holy Spirit: as it was in the beginning, is now, and shall be for ever.   Amen.

Lord, deepen our friendship with you, that our friendship with one another may be strong and true.   Amen.

ALTERNATIVE REFRAIN:
> *The commandments of the Lord are true:*
> *And rejoice the heart.*

The Spirit of truth

John 16:1–15

In the name of the Father, and of the Son, and of the Holy Spirit. Amen.

Our Father . . .

'I have told you all this so that you may not fall away. They will expel you from the synagogues, and indeed the time is coming when anyone who kills you will think he is doing a holy service to God. They will do these things because they have never known either the Father or me. But I have told you all this, so that when the time for it comes you may remember that I told you.'

Blessed be Jesus, true God and true man.
Blessed be the name of Jesus.

SILENCE

'I did not tell you this from the beginning, because I was with you; but now I am going to the one who sent me. Not one of you asks, "Where are you going?". Yet you are sad at heart because I have told you this. Still, I am telling you the truth: it is for your own good that I am going, because unless I go, the Paraclete will not come to you; but if I go, I will send him to you.'

REFRAIN FOLLOWED BY SILENCE

'And when he comes, he will show the world how wrong it was, about sin, and about who was in the right, and about judgement; about sin: in that they refuse to believe in me; about who was in the right: in that I am going to the Father and you will see me no more; about judgement: in that the prince of this world is already condemned.'

REFRAIN FOLLOWED BY SILENCE

'I still have many things to say to you but they would be too much for you to bear now. However, when the Spirit of truth comes he will lead you to the complete truth, since he will not be speaking of his own accord, but will say only what he has been told; and he will reveal to you the things to come.'

REFRAIN FOLLOWED BY SILENCE

'He will glorify me, since all he reveals to you will be taken from what is mine. Everything the Father has is mine; that is why I said: all he reveals to you will be taken from what is mine.'

REFRAIN FOLLOWED BY SILENCE

Glory to the Father, and to the Son, and to the Holy Spirit: as it was in the beginning, is now, and shall be for ever.   Amen.

Cleanse us, O Lord, with the fire of the Holy Spirit, that our love for you and one another may be in purity and truth.   Amen.

ALTERNATIVE REFRAIN:
When the Spirit of truth is come:
He will lead you into all truth.

Your joy will be full

In the name of the Father, and of the Son, and of the Holy Spirit.   Amen.

Our Father . . .

'In a short time you will no longer see me, and then a short time later you will see me again. Then some of his disciples said to one another, 'What does he mean, "In a short time you will no longer see me, and then a short time later you will see me again," and "I am going to the Father"? What is this "short time"? We don't know what he means.' Jesus knew that they wanted to question him, so he said, 'You are asking one another what I meant by saying, "In a short time you will no longer see me, and then a short time later you will see me again." '

> *Blessed be Jesus, true God and true man.*
> *Blessed be the name of Jesus.*

SILENCE

'In all truth I tell you, you will be weeping and wailing while the world will rejoice; you will be sorrowful, but your sorrow will turn to joy. A woman in childbirth suffers, because her time has come; but when she has given birth to the child she forgets the suffering in her joy that a human being has been born into the world. So it is with you: you are sad now, but I shall see you again, and your hearts will be full of joy, and that joy no one shall take from you.'

REFRAIN FOLLOWED BY SILENCE

'When that day comes, you will not ask me any questions. In all truth I tell you, anything you ask from the Father he will grant in my name. Until now you have not asked anything in my name. Ask and you will receive, and so your joy will be complete.'

REFRAIN FOLLOWED BY SILENCE

'I have been telling you these things in veiled language. The hour is coming when I shall no longer speak to you in veiled language but tell you about the Father in plain words. When that day comes you will ask in my name; and I do not say that I shall pray to the Father for you, because the Father himself loves you for loving me and believing that I came from God. I came from the Father and have come into the world and now I am leaving the world to go to the Father.'

REFRAIN FOLLOWED BY SILENCE

His disciples said, 'Now you are speaking plainly and not using veiled language. Now we see that you know everything and need not wait for questions to be put into words; because of this we believe that you came from God.' Jesus answered them, 'Do you believe at last? Listen; the time will come – indeed it has come already – when you are going to be scattered, each going his own way and leaving me alone. And yet I am not alone, because the Father is with me. I have told you all this so that you may find peace in me. In the world you will have hardship, but be courageous: I have conquered the world.'

REFRAIN FOLLOWED BY SILENCE

Glory to the Father, and to the Son, and to the Holy Spirit: as it was in the beginning, is now, and shall be for ever.   Amen.

Lord, in times of darkness, enable us to wait patiently until you reveal yourself again and fill our hearts with joy.   Amen.

ALTERNATIVE REFRAIN:
> *I will turn the wilderness into pools:*
> *And dry lands into springs of water.*

That they may be one

John 17:1–24

In the name of the Father, and of the Son, and of the Holy Spirit. Amen.

Our Father . . .

After saying this, Jesus raised his eyes to heaven and said, 'Father, the hour has come: glorify your Son so that your Son may glorify you; so that, just as you have given him power over all humanity, he may give eternal life to all those you have entrusted to him. And eternal life is this: to know you, the only true God, and Jesus Christ whom you have sent.'

> *Blessed be Jesus, true God and true man.*
> *Blessed be the name of Jesus.*

SILENCE

'I have glorified you on earth by finishing the work that you gave me to do. Now, Father, glorify me with that glory I had with you before ever the world existed. I have revealed your name to those whom you took from the world to give me. They were yours and you gave them to me, and they have kept your word. Now at last they have recognised that all you have given me comes from you for I have given them the teaching you gave to me, and they have indeed accepted it and know for certain that I came from you, and have believed that it was you who sent me.'

REFRAIN FOLLOWED BY SILENCE

'It is for them that I pray. I am not praying for the world but for those you have given me, because they belong to you. All I have is yours and all you have is mine, and in them I am glorified. I am no longer in the world, but they are in the world, and I am coming to you. Holy Father, keep those you have given me true to your name, so that they may be one like us. While I was with them, I kept those you had given me true to your name. I have watched over them and not one

78

is lost except one who was destined to be lost, and this was to fulfil the scriptures.'

REFRAIN FOLLOWED BY SILENCE

'But now I am coming to you and I say these things in the world to share my joy with them to the full. I passed your word on to them, and the world hated them, because they belong to the world no more than I belong to the world. I am not asking you to remove them from the world, but to protect them from the Evil One. They do not belong to the world any more than I belong to the world. Consecrate them in the truth; your word is truth. As you sent me into the world, I have sent them into the world, and for their sake I consecrate myself so that they too may be consecrated in truth.'

REFRAIN FOLLOWED BY SILENCE

'I pray not only for these but also for those who through their teaching will come to believe in me. May they all be one, just as, Father, you are in me and I am in you, so that they also may be in us, so that the world may believe it was you who sent me. I have given them the glory you gave to me, that they may be one as we are one. With me in them and you in me, may they be so perfected in unity that the world will recognise that it was you who sent me and that you have loved them as you loved me. Father, I want those you have given me to be with me where I am, so that they may always see my glory which you have given me because you loved me before the foundation of the world.'

REFRAIN FOLLOWED BY SILENCE

Glory to the Father, and to the Son, and to the Holy Spirit: as it was in the beginning, is now, and shall be for ever.   Amen.

Grant, Lord, to your people the unity of the Spirit in the bond of peace.   Amen.

ALTERNATIVE REFRAIN:
This is life eternal:
To know you, the true God, and Jesus Christ whom you have sent.

Gethsemane

John 18:1–11

In the name of the Father, and of the Son, and of the Holy Spirit. Amen.

Our Father . . .

After he had said all this, Jesus left with his disciples and crossed the Kidron valley where there was a garden into which he went with his disciples.

> *Blessed be Jesus, true God and true man.*
> *Blessed be the name of Jesus.*

SILENCE

Judas the traitor knew the place also, since Jesus had often met his disciples there, so Judas brought the cohort to this place together with guards sent by the chief priests and the Pharisees, all with lanterns and torches and weapons.

REFRAIN FOLLOWED BY SILENCE

Knowing everything that was to happen to him, Jesus came forward and said, 'Who are you looking for?' They answered, 'Jesus the Nazarene.' He said, 'I am he.'

REFRAIN FOLLOWED BY SILENCE

Now Judas the traitor was standing among them. When Jesus said to them, 'I am he,' they moved back and fell on the ground. He asked them a second time, 'Who are you looking for?' They said, 'Jesus the Nazarene.' Jesus replied, 'I have told you that I am he. If I am the one you are looking for, let these others go.' This was to fulfil the words he had spoken, 'Not one of those you gave me have I lost.'

REFRAIN FOLLOWED BY SILENCE

Simon Peter, who had a sword, drew it and struck the high priest's servant, cutting off his right ear. The servant's name was Malchus. Jesus said to Peter, 'Put your sword back in its scabbard; am I not to drink the cup that the Father has given me?'

REFRAIN FOLLOWED BY SILENCE

Glory to the Father, and to the Son, and to the Holy Spirit: as it was in the beginning, is now, and shall be for ever.   Amen.

Save us, Lord, in the time of trial, and deliver us from the Evil One.   Amen.

ALTERNATIVE REFRAIN:
Though I walk through the valley of the shadow of death:
I will fear no evil, for you are with me.

The ordeal of Peter

John 18:12–32

In the name of the Father, and of the Son, and of the Holy Spirit. Amen.

Our Father . . .

The cohort and its tribune and the Jewish guards seized Jesus and bound him. They took him first to Annas, because Annas was the father-in-law of Caiaphas, who was high priest that year. It was Caiaphas who had counselled the Jews, 'It is better for one man to die for the people.'

> *Blessed be Jesus, true God and true man.*
> *Blessed be the name of Jesus.*

SILENCE

Simon Peter, with another disciple, followed Jesus. This disciple, who was known to the high priest, went with Jesus into the high priest's palace, but Peter stayed outside the door. So the other disciple, the one known to the high priest, went out, spoke to the door-keeper and brought Peter in. The girl on duty at the door said to Peter, 'Aren't you another of that man's disciples?' He answered, 'I am not.' Now it was cold, and the servants and guards had lit a charcoal fire and were standing there warming themselves; so Peter stood there too, warming himself with the others.

REFRAIN FOLLOWED BY SILENCE

The high priest questioned Jesus about his disciples and his teaching. Jesus answered, 'I have spoken openly for all the world to hear; I have always taught in the synagogue and in the Temple where all the Jews meet together; I have said nothing in secret. Why ask me? Ask my hearers what I taught; they know what I said.' At these words, one of the guards standing by gave Jesus a slap in the face, saying, 'Is that the way you answer the high priest?' Jesus replied, 'If there is some offence in what I said, point it out; but if not, why do

82

you strike me?' Then Annas sent him, bound, to Caiaphas the high priest.

REFRAIN FOLLOWED BY SILENCE

As Simon Peter stood there warming himself, someone said to him, 'Aren't you another of his disciples?' He denied it, saying, 'I am not.' One of the high priest's servants, a relation of the man whose ear Peter had cut off, said, 'Didn't I see you in the garden with him?' Again Peter denied it; and at once a cock crew.

REFRAIN FOLLOWED BY SILENCE

They then led Jesus from the house of Caiaphas to the Praetorium. It was now morning. They did not go into the Praetorium themselves to avoid becoming defiled and unable to eat the Passover. So Pilate came outside to them and said, 'What charge do you bring against this man?' They replied, 'If he were not a criminal, we should not have handed him over to you.' Pilate said, 'Take him yourselves, and try him by your own Law.' The Jews answered, 'We are not allowed to put a man to death.' This was to fulfil the words Jesus had spoken indicating the way he was going to die.

REFRAIN FOLLOWED BY SILENCE

Glory to the Father, and to the Son, and to the Holy Spirit: as it was in the beginning, is now, and shall be for ever.   Amen.

We ask you, Lord, to pour your grace upon us that your strength may be made perfect in our weakness.   Amen.

ALTERNATIVE REFRAIN:
> *Lord, have mercy upon us:*
> *Christ, have mercy upon us.*

Jesus before Pilate

John 18:33–19:11

In the name of the Father, and of the Son, and of the Holy Spirit. Amen.

Our Father . . .

So Pilate went back into the Praetorium and called Jesus to him and asked him, 'Are you the king of the Jews?' Jesus replied, 'Do you ask this of your own accord, or have others said it to you about me?' Pilate answered, 'Am I a Jew? It is your own people and the chief priests who have handed you over to me: what have you done?' Jesus replied, 'Mine is not a kingdom of this world; if my kingdom were of this world, my men would have fought to prevent my being surrendered to the Jews. As it is, my kingdom does not belong here.'

Blessed be Jesus, true God and true man.
Blessed be the name of Jesus.

SILENCE

Pilate said, 'So, then you are a king?' Jesus answered, 'It is you who say that I am a king. I was born for this, I came into the world for this, to bear witness to the truth; and all who are on the side of truth listen to my voice.' 'Truth?' said Pilate. 'What is that?' And so saying he went out again to the Jews and said, 'I find no case against him. But according to a custom of yours I should release one prisoner at the Passover; would you like me, then, to release for you the king of the Jews?' At this they shouted; 'Not this man,' they said, 'but Barabbas.' Barabbas was a bandit.

REFRAIN FOLLOWED BY SILENCE

Pilate then had Jesus taken away and scourged; and after this, the soldiers twisted some thorns into a crown and put it on his head and dressed him in a purple robe. They kept coming up to him and saying, 'Hail, king of the Jews!', and slapping him in the face.

REFRAIN FOLLOWED BY SILENCE

84

Pilate came outside again and said to them, 'Look, I am going to bring him out to you to let you see that I find no case against him.' Jesus then came out wearing the crown of thorns and the purple robe. Pilate said, 'Here is the man.' When they saw him, the chief priests and the guards shouted, 'Crucify him! Crucify him!' Pilate said, 'Take him yourselves and crucify him: I find no case against him.' The Jews replied, 'We have a Law, and according to that Law he ought to be put to death, because he has claimed to be Son of God.'

REFRAIN FOLLOWED BY SILENCE

When Pilate heard them say this his fears increased. Re-entering the Praetorium, he said to Jesus, 'Where do you come from?' But Jesus made no answer. Pilate then said to him, 'Are you refusing to speak to me? Surely you know I have power to release you and I have power to crucify you?' Jesus replied, 'You would have no power over me at all if it had not been given you from above; that is why the one who handed me over to you has the greater guilt.'

REFRAIN FOLLOWED BY SILENCE

Glory to the Father, and to the Son, and to the Holy Spirit: as it was in the beginning, is now, and shall be for ever.   Amen.

Lord, you know our weakness; enable us to conquer the fear which makes us betray the truth.   Amen.

ALTERNATIVE REFRAIN:
The Lord is near to all who call upon him:
To all who call upon him in truth.

Jesus is crucified

John 19:12–30

In the name of the Father, and of the Son, and of the Holy Spirit. Amen.

Our Father . . .

From that moment Pilate was anxious to set him free, but the Jews shouted, 'If you set him free you are no friend of Caesar's; anyone who makes himself king is defying Caesar.' Hearing these words, Pilate had Jesus brought out, and seated himself on the chair of judgement at a place called the Pavement; in Hebrew Gabbatha. It was the Day of Preparation, about the sixth hour. 'Here is your king,' said Pilate to the Jews. But they shouted, 'Away with him, away with him, crucify him!' Pilate said, 'Shall I crucify your king?' The chief priests answered, 'We have no king except Caesar.' So at that Pilate handed him over to them to be crucified.

> *Blessed be Jesus, true God and true man.*
> *Blessed be the name of Jesus.*

SILENCE

They then took charge of Jesus, and carrying his own cross he went out to the Place of the Skull or, as it is called in Hebrew, Golgotha, where they crucified him with two others, one on either side, Jesus being in the middle. Pilate wrote out a notice and had it fixed to the cross; it ran 'Jesus the Nazarene, King of the Jews'. This notice was read by many of the Jews, because the place where Jesus was crucified was near the city, and the writing was in Hebrew, Latin and Greek. So the Jewish chief priests said to Pilate, 'You should not write "King of the Jews", but that the man said, "I am King of the Jews". Pilate answered, 'What I have written, I have written.'

REFRAIN FOLLOWED BY SILENCE

When the soldiers had finished crucifying Jesus they took his clothing and divided it into four shares, one for each soldier. His undergarment was seamless, woven in one piece from neck to hem; so they said to one another, 'Instead of tearing it, let's throw dice to decide who is to have it.' In this way the words of scripture were fulfilled: *They divide my garments among them and cast lots for my clothes.* That is what the soldiers did.

REFRAIN FOLLOWED BY SILENCE

Near the cross of Jesus stood his mother and his mother's sister, Mary the wife of Clopas, and Mary of Magdala. Seeing his mother and the disciple whom he loved standing near her, Jesus said to his mother, 'Woman, this is your son.' Then to the disciple he said, 'This is your mother.' And from that hour the disciple took her into his home.

REFRAIN FOLLOWED BY SILENCE

After this, Jesus knew that everything had now been completed and, so that the scripture should be completely fulfilled, he said, *I am thirsty.* A jar full of sour wine stood there; so, putting a sponge soaked in the wine on a hyssop stick, they held it up to his mouth. After Jesus had taken the wine he said, 'It is fulfilled'; and bowing his head he gave up his spirit.

REFRAIN FOLLOWED BY SILENCE

Glory to the Father, and to the Son, and to the Holy Spirit: as it was in the beginning, is now, and shall be for ever.   Amen.

Into your hands we commend our spirits, for you have redeemed us, O Lord, our God of truth.   Amen.

ALTERNATIVE REFRAIN:
> *Blessed are the dead which die in the Lord:*
> *They shall rest from their labours.*

Burial

John 19:31–42

In the name of the Father, and of the Son, and of the Holy Spirit. Amen.

Our Father . . .

It was the Day of Preparation, and to avoid the bodies' remaining on the cross during the Sabbath – since that Sabbath was a day of special solemnity – the Jews asked Pilate to have the legs broken and the bodies taken away. Consequently the soldiers came and broke the legs of the first man who had been crucified with him and then of the other.

> *Blessed be Jesus, true God and true man.*
> *Blessed be the name of Jesus.*

SILENCE

When they came to Jesus, they saw he was already dead, and so instead of breaking his legs one of the soldiers pierced his side with a lance; and immediately there came out blood and water.

REFRAIN FOLLOWED BY SILENCE

This is the evidence of one who saw it – true evidence, and he knows that what he says is true – and he gives it so that you may believe as well. Because all this happened to fulfil the words of scripture: *Not one bone of his will be broken*; and again, in another place scripture says: *They will look to the one whom they have pierced.*

REFRAIN FOLLOWED BY SILENCE

After this, Joseph of Arimathea, who was a disciple of Jesus – though a secret one because he was afraid of the Jews – asked Pilate to let him remove the body of Jesus. Pilate gave permission, so they came and took it away. Nicodemus came as well – the same one who had first come to Jesus at night-time – and he brought a mixture of myrrh and aloes, weighing about a hundred pounds. They took the body of Jesus and bound it in linen cloths with the spices, following the Jewish burial custom.

REFRAIN FOLLOWED BY SILENCE

At the place where he had been crucified there was a garden, and in this garden a new tomb in which no one had yet been buried. Since it was the Jewish Day of Preparation and the tomb was nearby, they laid Jesus there.

REFRAIN FOLLOWED BY SILENCE

Glory to the Father, and to the Son, and to the Holy Spirit: as it was in the beginning, is now, and shall be for ever.   Amen.

By your agony and trial; by your cross and passion; and by your precious death and burial, good Lord, deliver us.   Amen.

ALTERNATIVE REFRAIN:
> *If we die with him:*
> *We shall also rise with him.*

The resurrection

John 20:1–18

In the name of the Father, and of the Son, and of the Holy Spirit. Amen.

Our Father . . .

It was very early on the first day of the week and still dark, when Mary of Magdala came to the tomb. She saw that the stone had been moved away from the tomb and came running to Simon Peter and the other disciple, the one whom Jesus loved. 'They have taken the Lord out of the tomb,' she said, 'and we don't know where they have put him.'

> *Blessed be Jesus, true God and true man.*
> *Blessed be the name of Jesus.*

SILENCE

So Peter set out with the other disciple to go to the tomb. They ran together, but the other disciple, running faster than Peter, reached the tomb first; he bent down and saw the linen cloths lying on the ground,* but did not go in. Simon Peter, following him, also came up, went into the tomb, saw the linen cloths lying on the ground and also the cloth that had been over his head; this was not with the linen cloths but rolled up in a place by itself. Then the other disciple who had reached the tomb first also went in; he saw and he believed. Till this moment they had still not understood the scripture, that he must rise from the dead. The disciples then went back home.

REFRAIN FOLLOWED BY SILENCE

---

* The words 'on the ground' are not in the Greek and there is no hint of a natural disturbance of the cloths as the added words might suggest. If the enwrapped body had been laid on a ledge – as is generally supposed – then we are left to understand that the cloths remained where the body had been; 'not dishevelled and disarranged, they were lying there *still in their folds* – that is what the Greek means'. See William Barclay, 'The Gospel of John', The Daily Study Bible (Edinburgh, The Saint Andrew Press 1955).

But Mary was standing outside near the tomb, weeping. Then, as she wept, she stooped to look inside, and saw two angels in white sitting where the body of Jesus had been, one at the head, the other at the feet. They said, 'Woman, why are you weeping?' 'They have taken my Lord away,' she replied, 'and I don't know where they have put him.'

REFRAIN FOLLOWED BY SILENCE

As she said this she turned round and saw Jesus standing there, though she did not realise that it was Jesus. Jesus said to her, 'Woman, why are you weeping? Who are you looking for?' Supposing him to be the gardener, she said, 'Sir, if you have taken him away, tell me where you have put him, and I will go and remove him.' Jesus said, 'Mary!' She turned round then and said to him in Hebrew, 'Rabbuni!' – which means Master. Jesus said to her, 'Do not cling to me, because I have not yet ascended to the Father. But go and find my brothers, and tell them: I am ascending to my Father and your Father, to my God and your God.'

REFRAIN FOLLOWED BY SILENCE

So Mary of Magdala told the disciples, 'I have seen the Lord,' and that he had said these things to her.

REFRAIN FOLLOWED BY SILENCE

Glory to the Father, and to the Son, and to the Holy Spirit: as it was in the beginning, is now, and shall be for ever.   Amen.

Father, grant that we being risen with Christ may seek those things which are above, and may at the last be raised to live with him in the fullness of joy in your eternal kingdom.   Amen.

ALTERNATIVE REFRAIN:
The Lord is risen from the tomb:
He is risen indeed.

The appearance behind closed doors

John 20:19–29

In the name of the Father, and of the Son, and of the Holy Spirit. Amen.

Our Father . . .

In the evening of that same day, the first day of the week, the doors were closed in the room where the disciples were, for fear of the Jews. Jesus came and stood among them. He said to them, 'Peace be with you,' and, after saying this, he showed them his hands and his side.

> *Blessed be Jesus, true God and true man.*
> *Blessed be the name of Jesus.*

SILENCE

The disciples were filled with joy at seeing the Lord, and he said to them again, 'Peace be with you. As the Father sent me, so am I sending you.' After saying this he breathed on them and said, 'Receive the Holy Spirit. If you forgive anyone's sins, they are forgiven; if you retain anyone's sins, they are retained.'

REFRAIN FOLLOWED BY SILENCE

Thomas, called the Twin, who was one of the Twelve, was not with them when Jesus came. So the other disciples said to him, 'We have seen the Lord,' but he answered, 'Unless I can see the holes that the nails made in his hands and can put my finger into the holes they made, and unless I can put my hand into his side, I refuse to believe.'

REFRAIN FOLLOWED BY SILENCE

Eight days later the disciples were in the house again and Thomas was with them. The doors were closed, but Jesus came in and stood among them. 'Peace be with you,' he said. Then he spoke to Thomas, 'Put your finger here; look, here are my hands. Give me your hand, put it into my side. Do not be unbelieving any more but believe.' Thomas replied, 'My Lord and my God.'

REFRAIN FOLLOWED BY SILENCE

Jesus said to him, 'You believe because you can see me. Blessed are those who have not seen and yet believe.'

REFRAIN FOLLOWED BY SILENCE

Glory to the Father, and to the Son, and to the Holy Spirit: as it was in the beginning, is now, and shall be for ever.   Amen.

Lord, we believe that you are the Resurrection and the Life: come to us in our weakness and fill our lives with the strength and glory of your own risen life.   Amen.

ALTERNATIVE REFRAIN:
> *Blessed be Jesus, the Resurrection and the Life:*
> *Blessed be the name of Jesus.*

The appearance by the lake

John 21:1–14

In the name of the Father, and of the Son, and of the Holy Spirit.   Amen.

Our Father . . .

Later on, Jesus revealed himself again to the disciples. It was by the Sea of Tiberias, and it happened like this: Simon Peter, Thomas called the Twin, Nathaniel from Cana in Galilee, the sons of Zebedee and two more of his disciples were together. Simon Peter said, 'I'm going fishing.' They replied, 'We'll come with you.' They went out and got into the boat but caught nothing that night.

> *Blessed be Jesus, true God and true man.*
> *Blessed be the name of Jesus.*

SILENCE

When it was already light, there stood Jesus on the shore, though the disciples did not realise that it was Jesus. Jesus called out, 'Haven't you caught anything, friends?' And when they answered, 'No,' he said, 'Throw the net out to starboard and you'll find something.' So they threw the net out and could not haul it in because of the quantity of fish.

REFRAIN FOLLOWED BY SILENCE

The disciple whom Jesus loved said to Peter, 'It is the Lord.' At these words, 'It is the Lord,' Simon Peter tied his outer garment round him (for he had nothing on) and jumped into the water. The other disciples came on in the boat, towing the net with the fish; they were only about a hundred yards from land.

REFRAIN FOLLOWED BY SILENCE

As soon as they came ashore they saw that there was some bread there and a charcoal fire with fish cooking on it. Jesus said, 'Bring some of the fish you have just caught.' Simon

Peter went aboard and dragged the net ashore, full of big fish, one hundred and fifty-three of them; and in spite of there being so many the net was not broken.

REFRAIN FOLLOWED BY SILENCE

Jesus said to them, 'Come and have breakfast.' None of the disciples was bold enough to ask, 'Who are you?'; they knew quite well it was the Lord. Jesus then stepped forward, took the bread and gave it to them, and the same with the fish. This was the third time that Jesus revealed himself to the disciples after rising from the dead.

REFRAIN FOLLOWED BY SILENCE

Glory to the Father, and to the Son, and to the Holy Spirit: as it was in the beginning, is now, and shall be for ever.   Amen.

Come, Lord, with the dawning of the day, and make yourself known in the breaking of the bread.   Amen.

ALTERNATIVE REFRAIN:
   Christ is risen from the dead:
   And become the first-fruits of them that slept.

The restoration of Peter

John 21:15–25

In the name of the Father, and of the Son, and of the Holy Spirit.   Amen.

Our Father . . .

When they had eaten, Jesus said to Simon Peter, 'Simon son of John, do you love me more than these others do?' He answered, 'Yes, Lord, you know I love you.' Jesus said to him, 'Feed my lambs.'

> *Blessed be Jesus, true God and true man.*
> *Blessed be the name of Jesus.*

SILENCE

A second time he said to him, 'Simon son of John, do you love me?' He replied, 'Yes, Lord, you know I love you.' Jesus said to him, 'Look after my sheep.'

REFRAIN FOLLOWED BY SILENCE

Then he said to him a third time, 'Simon son of John, do you love me?' Peter was hurt that he asked him a third time, 'Do you love me?' and said, 'Lord, you know everything; you know I love you.' Jesus said to him, 'Feed my sheep. In all truth I tell you, when you were young you put on your own belt and walked where you liked; but when you grow old you will stretch out your hands, and somebody else will put a belt round you and take you where you would rather not go.' In these words he indicated the kind of death by which Peter would give glory to God. After this he said, 'Follow me.'

REFRAIN FOLLOWED BY SILENCE

Peter turned and saw the disciple whom Jesus loved following them – the one who had leant back close to his chest at the supper and had said to him, 'Lord, who is it that will betray you?' Seeing him, Peter said to Jesus, 'What about him, Lord?' Jesus answered, 'If I want him to stay behind till I come, what does it matter to you? You are to follow me.' The rumour then went out among the brothers that this disciple would not die. Yet Jesus had not said to Peter, 'He will not die,' but, 'If I want him to stay behind till I come.'

REFRAIN FOLLOWED BY SILENCE

This disciple is the one who vouches for these things and has written them down, and we know that his testimony is true. There was much else that Jesus did; if it were written down in detail, I do not suppose the world itself would hold all the books that would be written.

REFRAIN FOLLOWED BY SILENCE

Glory to the Father, and to the Son, and to the Holy Spirit; as it was in the beginning, is now, and shall be for ever.   Amen.

Lord, as we grow older you choose our ways more and more. Enable us to submit gladly to your wisdom, knowing that in your will lies our peace and the glory of your name.   Amen.

ALTERNATIVE REFRAIN:
> *The Father himself loves you:*
> *Because you have loved me.*

APPENDIX I

Introduction to the Gospel of St John

DATE, AUTHORSHIP AND FORM OF THE GOSPEL

Tradition almost unanimously names John the apostle, the son of Zebedee, as the author. Before AD 150 the book was known and used by Ignatius of Antioch, Papias, Justin and the author of the *Odes of Solomon*, and the first explicit testimony is by Irenaeus, *c*. 180: 'Last of all John, too, the disciple of the Lord who leant against his breast, himself brought out a gospel while he was in Ephesus.' The Gospel itself has much supporting evidence, apart from its claim to be the work of an eye-witness who was a beloved disciple of the Lord: its vocabulary and style betray its semitic origin, it is familiar with Jewish customs and with the topography of Palestine, and its author is evidently a close friend of Peter.

It was published not by John himself but by his disciples after his death, and it is possible that in this Gospel we have the end-stage of a slow process that has brought together not only component parts of different ages but also corrections, additions and sometimes more than one revision of the same discourse. The arrangement of the Gospel is not always easy to explain, but it is clear that the author attaches special importance to the Jewish liturgical feasts which punctuate his narrative; the following analysis can be made:

Prologue (1:1–18)

I *First week* of the messianic ministry, ending with the first miracle at Cana (1:19—2:11)

II *First Passover* with accompanying events, ending with the second miracle at Cana (2:12—4:54)

III *Sabbath 'of the paralytic'* (5:1–47)

IV *The Passover 'of the bread of life'* and its discourse (6:1–71)

V *The feast of Tabernacles* and the man born blind (7:1—10:21)

VI *The feast of Dedication* and the raising of Lazarus (10:22—11:54)

VII *Week of the Passion* and the crucifixion Passover (11:55—19:42)

VIII *The resurrection* and week of appearances (20:1–29)

IX *Appendix*: the Church and Christ's return (ch. 21)

This division suggests that Christ not only fulfilled the Jewish liturgy but in doing so brought it to an end.

SPECIAL CHARACTERISTICS OF THE GOSPEL

The Fourth Gospel is concerned to bring out the significance of all that Christ did and said. The things that he did were 'signs', and the meaning of them, hidden at first, could be understood only after his glorification; the things he said had a deeper meaning not perceived at the time but understood only after the Spirit who spoke in the name of the risen Christ had come to 'lead' his disciples 'into all truth'. The Gospel is revelation at this stage of development.

The whole of John's thought is dominated by the mystery of the incarnation, from the Prologue with which the book opens. Here the revelation of Christ's glory, which in the Synoptic Gospels is associated primarily with his return at the end of time, has a new interpretation: judgement is working here and now in the soul, and eternal life (John's counterpart to the 'kingdom' of the Synoptic Gospels) is made to be something actually present, already in the possession of those who have faith. God's victory over evil, his salvation of the world, is already guaranteed by Christ's resurrection in glory.*

*Taken from the Jerusalem Bible, published and copyright 1966, 1967 and 1968 by Darton, Longman & Todd Ltd and Doubleday & Co Inc.

APPENDIX II

Two prayers from Medjugorje

Jesus, we know that you are merciful and that you have offered your heart for us. It is crowned with thorns and with our sins.

We know that you implore us constantly so that we do not go astray. Jesus, remember us when we are in sin. By means of your heart make all men love one another. Make hatred disappear from among men.

Show us your love. We all love you and want you to protect us with your shepherd's heart and free us from every sin.

Jesus, enter into every heart! Knock, knock at the door of our heart. Be patient and never desist. We are still closed because we have not understood your love.

Knock continuously. O good Jesus, make us open our hearts to you at least in the moment when we remember your Passion suffered for us. Amen.

A PRAYER FOR A SICK PERSON

O, my God, this sick person who is before you came to ask you for that which he sees as most important to him.

But you, God, bring into his heart these words: 'It is important to be healthy in soul!'

Lord, let your holy will be done upon him in everything! If you will it, let him receive the healing. If it is your will, let him continue to bear his cross.

I pray to you for us who are praying to you for him; purify our hearts that we may become worthy that you give your holy graces through us.

Guard him and lighten his pains. Let your holy will continue to be fulfilled upon him, and grant that your holy love manifest itself in him. Help him to carry his cross courageously.

(After this prayer, say the *Glory to the Father* . . . three times.)

NOTE

These two prayers were given by Mary to Jelena Vasilj (born 14 May 1972) of Medjugorje. The first was given on 28 November 1983 when she was eleven years old, the second on 22 June 1985. Jelena is not one of the six young people referred to in the Introduction (see page ix), but with another girl she is able to 'see our Lady with her heart' and converse with her. The prayers are translated from the Croatian in which they were given. The quotations relating to peace and prayer in the Introduction were also given to Jelena.

APPENDIX III

A note on silent prayer

Some may find it helpful if a few words are said about silence in prayer, since every meditation asks this of the reader. If silence is employed simply in desiring God, it is enough and we are truly at prayer. We can extend that thought and say that whatever we are doing, if the desire for God is present, we are indeed praying. St Augustine argues that it is only in understanding prayer in this way that we can fulfil St Paul's command to pray without ceasing. And so he writes, 'Your very desire is itself your prayer; if your desire is continued so is your prayer also.'

Could we but grasp this, silent prayer would become very simple; that does not mean that it will not be demanding. You take up your position, you allow thoughts and memories to drop away – which you do by not paying deliberate attention to them – you allow your unwanted bodily tensions to be released, and you simply desire God. It may help to repeat the refrain in the book (or another) over and over again in the silence (or aloud if you are alone, for the essence is the silence of the heart before God and not the absence of the voice) and if, after a time, what you are doing appears meaningless, you ask yourself one question only: 'Do I desire God?' Perhaps you will tell God that he already knows your desire, or ask him to renew it or strengthen it. If you are simply sitting in the silence and using no words, not even in the heart, the procedure is the same. Whenever your state seems pointless or a waste of time, ask only one question: 'Do I desire God?' On the answer to that, everything depends. Even so, if all you believe that you can truly say is that you desire to desire God, that is enough. God takes us from where we are and he will do the rest.

This is not to say that every period will be spent in this way; the Holy Spirit is our guide here as at all times. On another day, or at another stage, the drawing may be simply to rest in God as a child in its mother's arms and to let God bear us and enfold us in his love. Here is the more passive side of prayer. Prayer is an ongoing process; it might be described as a holding on to God until we move into the knowledge that we are being held.